BIG BUSINESS THINKING TO HELP YOU
GROW EXPONENTIALLY

BIG
LITTLE
BUSINESS

JAYNE ARLETT

FOREWORD BY DR GLEN RICHARDS,
SHARK TANK AUSTRALIA INVESTOR

First published by Ultimate World Publishing 2020
Copyright © 2020 Jayne Arlett

ISBN

Paperback: 978-1-922497-38-3
Ebook: 978-1-922497-39-0

Jayne Arlett has asserted her rights under the Copyright, Designs and Patents Act 1988 to be identified as the author of this work. The information in this book is based on the author's experiences and opinions. The publisher specifically disclaims responsibility for any adverse consequences which may result from use of the information contained herein. Permission to use information has been sought by the author. Any breaches will be rectified in further editions of the book. Some client identifying details have been changed to protect the privacy of individuals.

All rights reserved. No part of this publication may be reproduced, stored in or introduced into a retrieval system, or transmitted in any form, or by any means (electronic, mechanical, photocopying, recording or otherwise) without the prior written permission of the author. Any person who does any unauthorised act in relation to this publication may be liable to criminal prosecution and civil claims for damages. Enquiries should be made through the publisher.

Cover design: Vetta Productions
Layout and typesetting: Ultimate World Publishing
Editor: Marinda Wilkinson

Ultimate World Publishing
Diamond Creek,
Victoria Australia 3089
www.writeabook.com.au

What people are saying about Jayne Arlett and

BIG LITTLE BUSINESS

Jayne has a gift. Having watched her mentor start-up founders for several years, it never fails to impress how her humble yet at times confronting approach, gets them out of the chaos and back into the land of opportunity. Her ability to bring structure to those who are experiencing overwhelm and help them gain quick results is why she has become such a sought-after resource in the business world. *Big Little Business* provides us all with access to Jayne's extensive experience, providing a clear road map for anyone looking to create a high-performing, resilient and sustainable Little Business with the potential to go Big.

**Nicole Lucas, COO,
Smart Precinct North Queensland**

Jayne provided advice to prepare our national engineering company for adverse potential situations. We worked together in recovery from a major flood that impacted one of our offices and the advice and support she provided was very helpful in preparing ourselves for the COVID-19 pandemic. The learnings from this book will be invaluable for businesses of all sizes.

**Govinda Padney, CEO,
Rockfield Technologies**

I am 10 years into owning my own business and I just wish I could turn back time and begin it with this book in my back pocket! I consider myself a big picture, creative, exciting type, so the mundane details of my financials were never high on my priority list; largely because I didn't understand the power or importance of them. Money was always a struggle and I was working reactively, until Jayne showed me how numbers are the backbone to every decision I make. I now understand the numbers and use them to my advantage in planning and decision-making. It has also allowed me to build a business resilience plan and work on the front foot. Under Jayne's guidance, my business has expanded and is healthier than ever and I now LOVE the numbers. She also gave me a pay rise which makes me love her even more!

**Megan Colwell, Director,
First Things First and The Beauty & Body Bar**

Deep down, most small business owners will admit to having poor self-discipline when it comes to spending quality time working ON the business. *Big Little Business* is refreshingly motivating, with a battle plan and practical tips built into every chapter. The advice and guidance is easily adaptable for sole traders and microbusiness owners. I might start using a baseball hat at my workplace now too!

**Maree Adshead,
Queensland Small Business Commissioner**

As a microbusiness owner, Jayne has taught me how to be a marketer, a finance manager and the CEO of myself! I really love *Big Little Business* and know it will help many sole traders like myself to grow their business.

**Kareau McKey, CEO,
Kanga Training Townsville**

'Maths has never been my strong point' ... this mindset has followed me throughout my career as a business owner. After working with Jayne and reading this book I understand the important story that the numbers give me. Now, I really enjoy being a Financial Detective and have learnt to love my P&Ls! Implementing the simple strategies to read my financial reports, create a Magic Budget and cash flow forecast has allowed me to take charge and be in control of the business' money rather than it controlling me. My business has grown exponentially since Jayne and I have been working together. I'm excited that *Big Little Business* will allow so many other business owners to gain insight into the mechanics of business and it will help them grow too. A must-read for anyone in business.

**Joanna Murray, CEO,
Access Therapy Services**

We engaged Jayne to work with us to improve our understanding of the back end of our business, allowing us to feel more confident in the financial decisions we make. Jayne has an immense amount of experience in business, so to have someone to turn to for advice on how to move forward with opportunities has been invaluable. One of Jayne's key strengths is her wealth of experience and knowledge – and her ability to translate this across many different industries.

**Nicole Cross and Sam Wright, Directors,
Neighbourhood Productions**

We have engaged Jayne to assist us with high-level strategic conversations regarding the shaping of our tech start-up business for future regional, national and international growth. Jayne is a highly successful businesswomen in her own right with a deep appreciation for technology. She is particularly strong in Board Governance and the importance of building strategic enduring relationships, and brings a wealth of experience to these conversations. I strongly recommend Jayne's expertise and her book to any company, small through large.

Dr Jeffrey Loughran, CEO,
LiXiA

We worked with Jayne to look for other forms of income and revenue streams, to add pillars and diversify our business. We explored ways to commercialise our chocolate hazelnut spread Heavenly Hazel well beyond our local region. I'd recommend this book to any business that needs help to re-evaluate their business strategy, diversify and to grow and build their business sustainably.

Shelley Grainger, Director,
Nourishing Bites

Big Little Business is a must-read, not only for those interested in business success, but for anybody keen for some inspiration. Jayne Arlett has pulled together all the tips, tricks and strategies that you need to organise and grow your business.

Bettina Warburton, Editor,
Townsville Eye

Offering a breath of fresh air in the world of books designed for small business, *Big Little Business* has arrived. Within the book, business resilience and growth coach, Jayne Arlett shares her practical philosophy (and actionable advice) to building a successful, profitable, and enjoyable small business through the power of a big business mindset. It's one of the best guides I've read to building a business you'll love. Jayne's central message is that by taking achievable trusted steps, you will have a process to allow your business to be successful, avoiding much of the usual worry we typically associate with running a small business. This book offers a blueprint for small business success, and I am so grateful Jayne has shared her knowledge.

Dr Jo Lukins,
Director and Author

As a sole trader, I have been making it up as I go for eight years, juggling the different aspects of my growing freelance business reactively with no real structure or systems in place. Jayne's book has been life-changing, it was a real eye-opener and has definitely inspired me to change my thinking and overhaul the way I operate my business. After following her clear and actionable steps, the overwhelm is gone, I feel back in control and I have the confidence and knowledge to now take my business to the next level. I'm sure this book will help every business owner who reads it to implement positive changes into their business and life.

Marinda Wilkinson,
Copywriter and Editor, Vivid Words

The small business owner must juggle broad and diverse responsibilities for success. From planning and strategy, finance and accounting, marketing and sales, customer management, employee cultivation, and compliance and legal obligation – these are all tasks to master to reach goals of freedom and flexibility. *Big Little Business*, a handbook that draws on Jayne's years spent doing the hard yards and reaping the benefits. Her wealth of knowledge communicates in a style that cuts through to people in business. Like sitting with a wise friend, Jayne has balanced empathising with the journey of small business owners and offering firm, and guiding advice for success. I look forward to sharing *Big Little Business* with my clients to accelerate their success. Thank you, Jayne, for writing this important book.

**Joe Carey, Founding Director,
Carey Group of Companies**

DEDICATION

When I was a little girl, my paternal grandmother, my Nana always said I would be a teacher. Whilst I never had any desire to be a school teacher, I have spent my life teaching people. In my sports podiatry career, I taught people about their body mechanics and how to improve their sporting performance; and in my business career, I teach people about their business mechanics and how to improve their business performance.

Writing a book is a mammoth task that cannot be understood until you have gone down that path! Thank you to my wonderful family for the love and life lessons that have allowed me to develop the knowledge to share with others, and their unwavering support throughout my book writing journey.

Thank you to my many wonderful business clients who have urged me to write this book so others can grow their Little Businesses.

Thank you to my amazing friends and support crew that have given me feedback, cups of tea and encouragement throughout this writing process.

It's been a Big Little journey!

CONTENTS

What people are saying	iii
Dedication	ix
Foreword By Dr Glen Richards	xiii
Introduction: The Accidental Business Owner	xvii
Chapter 1: Big Little Business on a Page	1
Chapter 2: Big Business Thinking	11
Chapter 3: But Are You REALLY Making Money?	25
Chapter 4: The Financial Detective	37
Chapter 5: I See You!	51
Chapter 6: Roles, Goals and Process	63
Chapter 7: What's Holding You Back?	77
Chapter 8: Hold Your Course	89
Chapter 9: Roller-Coaster Junkie	97
Chapter 10: You Can Have It All – Just Not All At Once!	109
Chapter 11: Best Coffee Ever!	119
Chapter 12: Plan B	127
Afterword	133
About the Author	135

FOREWORD
By Dr Glen Richards

In December 1993, I arrived back in Australia after a two-year stint as a veterinarian in London. I travelled back to Townsville via a couple of flights and a six-week overland slog from Moscow to Hong Kong. After some final negotiations with banks, lawyers and sellers, and with the support of my parents, I commenced as a business owner in my one vet, three support staff veterinary hospital in Townsville.

At about the same time, a dynamic young sports podiatrist, Jayne Arlett, kicked off her practice just down the road. Her story and learnings in *Big Little Business* have some remarkable parallels with my own business journey, experiences and epiphanies. I blustered and bluffed my way through the first few years of business ownership, growing rapidly to multiple sites and with multiple staff. I made a lot of mistakes and burnt the candle at both ends, trying to be a great clinician and a great business owner. I was filling all the roles in the business, all the while maintaining (no doubt to the frustration of my employees and teammates) a control freak personality.

In 1998, after an extended period away from the business for my honeymoon, I came back to a practice in complete chaos

– revenue down 30%, key staff on the verge of resigning and clients leaving in droves. The epiphany: I was self-employed in an enterprise that had no structure, no discipline, no plans and was completely reliant on the founder (me) to keep all the plates twirling in the air. It was time to transition the business from being 'me' centric to being 'team and customer' centric and turn Greencross Vets into a serious business that other people may want to invest in or own.

During the next five years or so the stars started to align. I linked up with some wonderful multi-site practice owners from around Australia to form Vets Alliance with a mandate to share ideas and resources to support our practices. Soon after, a group of Queensland Vets established a veterinary cooperative (United Veterinary Services) to provide back office services to our frontline clinics. My Townsville group had grown to five veterinary practices and we had co-founded a large format pet store called Pet HQ as well as opened two veterinary practices in Shanghai, PR China. In 2007 our cooperative aligned with a couple of businessmen from the Gold Coast to bring together our 17 practices and a further 15 practices from around the country. We established Greencross Ltd (GXL) which became the first listed veterinary group in Australia.

From 2007 to 2014 I was the CEO and Managing Director of GXL. We grew from 32 clinics to over 120 clinics across Australia. During this time, I also was one of the founders and directors of Mammoth Holdings (Petbarn, City Farmers and Animates pet stores). The directors of both companies made the decision to merge the two companies in 2014 to create one of the largest consumer facing pet care companies in Australasia with over 200 pet stores, over 120 veterinary clinics and a combined workforce of over 5,000 employees and we reached a market capitalisation of $1.3 billion with a peak share price of $10.60. In the immortal words of Kenny Rogers, *'You've got to know when to hold 'em, know when to fold 'em.'* With a culture of success in the team, some of the most exciting innovations delivered for employees and clients in the veterinary industry, and a total shareholder return of over 1,500%, it was time to move from business owner to investor.

Over the last five years I teamed up with some wonderful founders at My Foot Dr, Balance Podiatry and Allsports Physiotherapy to establish a platform business, Healthia Ltd, to evolve a network of allied health practices across Australia. Healthia provides our local clinicians with coaching and enterprise-level corporate support to grow our practices, with a strong focus on education and leading-edge technologies so our partners can deliver high-quality clinical care for our patients.

One of the first practices our group targeted for acquisition was none other than Jayne Arlett's Townsville Podiatry Centre. It is one of Australia's largest podiatry clinics, with state-of-the-art facilities and methods. To paraphrase Victor Kiam, 'I liked the business so much – I bought it!'. The learnings found in this book are on display in this exceptional business.

Big Little Business is the essential business owners' guide to turning a Little Business into a smooth well-oiled and disciplined Big Business machine. Jayne is an exceptional and successful businesswoman and an outstanding business coach. Follow the steps below, and you will fast track the evolution from being a 'trapped and strapped' self-employee to a confident and strategic business owner/CEO whether you have a team of one or one hundred.

- Read *Big Little Business* cover to cover
- Make notes and key takeaways as you go
- Write up your action plan
- Find peer mentors, mentors and a business coach to assist you

Jayne's insights and suggestions coupled with good execution will move you from being dictated to by your business, to being a strategic and successful business owner.

I only wish I had read it back in 1993 – the learnings and insights would have transitioned me from control freak to thoughtful business owner/CEO about 15 years faster!

Dr Glen Richards,
Veterinary Surgeon, entrepreneur and Shark Tank Australia Investor

DR GLEN RICHARDS
Photo Credit Network Ten

Introduction

THE ACCIDENTAL BUSINESS OWNER

IT STARTS WITH A DREAM

On April 1st, 1976, a young university dropout and his friend set up a microbusiness in his father's garage. They needed money to establish the start-up of course, and so they sold their most valuable possessions (a beaten-up old Volkswagen and a fancy calculator) to fund their new venture.

Their dream was to build a computer for the people. One that was small and affordable enough that families could use it in their own homes – a revolutionary idea in those days! With around $1,500 in seed capital, they developed their first computer, dubbed Apple I. It was a world away from the sleek and stylish Apple Macs we know today, comprising of little more than a typewriter-like keyboard that you connected to your TV. Each computer was built by hand, and the company quickly developed a niche following of tech hobbyists. Still, it generated enough cash to get the business process off and running and to test and refine their ideas.

After selling 200 units of Apple I computers, in 1977 they introduced the ground-breaking and user-friendly Apple II. This was the first personal computer with colour graphics (six colours – hence the original Apple striped colour logo), a keyboard and a plastic casing based on contemporary kitchen appliance design. It was a game-changer in the computer industry and a tremendous success. Between 1977 and 1980, their revenue doubled every four months. In 1980 their revenue was $118million and the business went public. Apple has certainly had its ups and downs, like most businesses – although theirs have been more dramatic and more public than most!

Ultimately the business became a success because of the initial focus, vision and tenacity of its founders, Steve Jobs and Steve Wozniak. It started with a dream, but a dream that had a plan – and importantly, they had a single-minded focus and determination to execute that plan. This is how some (but not all) great businesses begin.

THE ACCIDENTAL BUSINESS OWNER

Most businesses have quite humble beginnings. I have had any number of clients say to me, 'I'm not like most people, I went into business because I was passionate about my (insert skill here), not because I wanted to make money!'. The truth is that MOST small businesses are driven by passion, creativity and a smattering of entrepreneurial spirit, at least in the early stages. The making money aspect is rarely the key driver for setting up a business initially – although it needs to come into the picture before too long!

My business journey was pretty ordinary in its origins. I graduated from university and after a few years, moved back to my home city. There were no jobs in my chosen field, and if I wanted to be able to stay, the only option I had was to set up my own business. I often call myself an *accidental business owner*. There was no grand plan. There was no great vision. However, I was good at what I did (being a sports podiatrist) and I quickly gained a solid reputation and became busy almost immediately.

I was just two years out of university when I set up my business with minimal life experience. I was a sole trader initially and grew the business quickly to the stage that I needed assistance. My first employee was in administration support, and that was a welcome relief. But I recall the first time I employed a full-time, professional employee on a significant salary. It almost destroyed my Little Business. Like many businesses, I had grown too fast, too soon and did not have any strategy in place to manage it. I had created a monster.

To enable me to pay my two employees, my rent and the many other business expenses, I worked a whole year with no salary for myself. I knew there had to be a better way.

I became a sponge, reading many, many business books and attending seminars and workshops to learn as much as I could about business. I began putting structure and strategy into my business and saw immediate results. I enjoyed the learnings, and business strategy eventually became second nature to me.

At the same time, I began a board career, serving as a company director on a variety of boards from tiny little not-for-profits, through to large, billion-dollar organisations. The one thing that I learned through this journey was that the strategies and mindsets that are used by Big Business and large corporations could also be applied to Little Businesses with significant effect.

My Little Business grew to become the largest podiatry practice in Australia at that time. I established new Little Businesses and bought underperforming existing Little Businesses, that I grew and on-sold. My original Little Business grew to a $10million Big Business, before we were bought out by a large, well-funded organisation for public listing.

IT'S NOT ALL FUN AND GAMES

But along the way, there were many highs and many lows. I've had too many sleepless nights to count, agonising over my decisions, not knowing how I would pay the bills, worrying if I might go bankrupt, being thrown into crisis mode when key team members moved on and much more. I had no Plan B to manage situations that went pear-shaped. I had problems with team management when I did not understand how to build a robust workplace culture in the early years, and that was to my detriment.

As time went by, my management and leadership skillset grew, and I realised employees are indeed the best asset that a business can have. Within my businesses, we developed a strong, positive culture with loyalty, commitment and a combined goal and drive to succeed at our core. We became an *employer of choice*, able to attract high-level, skilled, professional employees and retain them for a reasonable length of time.

Now, some years on, I work as a business development coach, helping others apply Big Business thinking to their own business to grow and develop it. I can guarantee you that most of the issues that you are having in your business, I have also had along my journey. I now spend my days helping people learn from my mistakes and do things better. Throughout this book, you will learn the tricks of the Big Business trade and find out how you too can grow exponentially.

So, where do we start? Well, your most pressing problem is a good place, but we will put some structure around that first. When I initially meet with business owners as their coach, we spend the first few meetings understanding their immediate business stressors; problems that need addressing before we can begin to set a solid Big Business strategy in place. The following three concerns are the most common:

1. **People Management**

   Around 80% of the businesses that I deal with indicate people management as one of their key issues. Their burning question is often, 'How do I get people to do what I want them to do?'.

2. **Minimal Reward**

   Too many business owners work extremely hard, putting in long hours in a stressful environment, for very little return. They see the money coming in, but it goes out the back door just as quick. Sometimes it feels like there is a minimal reward for all the hard work that you do in your own business.

3. **Business Bushfires**

   If you are constantly running around, putting out business bushfires all day, it robs you of your time and focus. You plan your day in the morning, but it's just problem after problem that needs your attention, or employees constantly interrupting with things that need to be dealt with. At the end of the day, you often wonder what you have achieved.

These issues (and many more) are covered throughout this book, as well as practical tips, tools and strategies to help your Little Business thrive. Here's an overview of what's to come:

Chapter 1: **Big Little Business on a Page**
>At the start of the journey, we revisit why you are in business and what is important to you. We cover how to build your own Big Little Business on a Page, a simple outline of your business that will keep you focused on what really matters and guide all elements of your strategic business growth.

Chapter 2: **Big Business Thinking**
>The most powerful thing you can do for your Little Business is to engage in strategic thinking, to create a Big Business structure and ask yourself the questions that will lead to growth. We will look at methods to structure your time and work strategically to prevent business bushfires before they occur.

Chapter 3: **But are you REALLY Making Money?**
>Here we explore the vanity vs. reality side of business and drill down on your profit centres to understand the true costs and profitability of the business and importantly, the areas of greatest opportunity for you.

Chapter 4: **The Financial Detective**
>This is where the magic happens! Numbers aren't sexy for a lot of people, but I happen to love them. I will help you to understand your finances in a meaningful way. We explore the critical markers you need to track and how to set yourself financial targets and stick to them. By the end of this process you might even enjoy reading your financial statements!

Chapter 5: **I See You!**
>Is your business full of your 'ideal' clients or customers or do some of them fall short of the mark? How well do you understand what an ideal client or customer looks like and

do you know how to reach them? In this chapter we really get to know your ideal client or customer and explain how best to spend your marketing dollar to attract them.

Chapter 6: **Roles, Goals and Process**

Employees can be your biggest asset and your biggest nightmare – largely based around how you structure and control this element of your business. We explore the systems you need to set your employees and your business up for success. It's not easy, but once you have your systems established and you have spent the time and energy to build a strong, positive team culture, you'll find it all starts to fall into place. This will increase your efficiency out of sight and provide a more stress-free work environment for both you and your team.

Chapter 7: **What's Holding You Back?**

How do you spend your time each day? How can you get all your jobs done? It's about understanding where your time is best spent and then prioritising those tasks. We will look at what your time suckers might be and how best to manage them.

Chapter 8: **Hold Your Course**

Throughout your business journey you will have times of rapid growth and without robust systems in place, things can get out of control very quickly. We look at the growth/consolidation model and how to steady the ship when it's all getting a bit choppy.

Chapter 9: **Roller-Coaster Junkie**

You will have your highs and lows in business, and you will learn resilience along the way! We look at tips and strategies to manage the roller-coaster ride of business, so you come out the end with a smile on your face.

Chapter 10: **You CAN Have it All! Just Not All at Once**
> That old work/life balance chestnut. There are many rewards to running your own business and flexibility to do the things you love has to be one of them – as long as you run your business right. We will explore whole-of-life goal setting and the different phases of your journey.

Chapter 11: **The Best Coffee Ever!**
> The value of mentorship – and coffee! It can be lonely being a business owner and having strong support mechanisms are invaluable. Understand what mentorship is and how to find the support you need.

Chapter 12: **Plan B**
> What do you do when things don't go as expected? Business does not always follow the path you have planned. Do you have a strategy in place to manage the downturns or the key threats to your business? Learn why I can't live without a good Plan B.

MICROBUSINESS AND SOLE TRADERS

Let me take a minute to talk to the sole traders out there. I work with businesses from initial start-up phase through to very large organisations. Sometimes the really Little Businesses think this strategy stuff just isn't relevant for them, they are *too little* and of course too *busy* to be taking time out of their frantic workday to *think*! But it is this very thing that makes all the difference in every business, no matter your size. In particular, microbusinesses and sole traders sometimes think they can skip the organisational structure piece, as it is only them that is available to fill every role – especially the people management element as they don't need to manage themselves! This is actually the most important role, because as a sole trader, your most valuable business resource and your most critical business risk is YOU! Trust me and trust the process and you will see your Little Business reap the rewards.

Now, let's get started!

Chapter 1

BIG LITTLE BUSINESS ON A PAGE

REMEMBER YOUR WHY

Let's begin at the beginning. Most people go into business because they're passionate about something. They might love cooking and people, so they open a café or a restaurant. They might be a professional service provider (medical/law/accounting) and want to work for themselves, so they open their own business. They might love homewares or fashion and open a retail shop. Whatever it is that you choose to do, there is generally passion, excitement and drive, in the early stages at least. Sometimes we open the business, and after that initial flush of enthusiasm, it all seems to get too tricky. The excitement and passion to be a business owner seem to die a little each day. It becomes a drudge to go to work, and you fear the problems you will have to face. You dread an employee coming to you with issues that only you can deal with – yet another business bushfire that demands your attention and time.

So, the first thing to do is to go back to basics and refocus on *why* you went into business in the first place. Let's develop your **Big Little Business on a Page**. Very few small businesses have a useful formal structure or strategy behind what they do. I certainly didn't for the initial years of my business journey! Some have a business plan that a consultant was paid to develop for them a few years ago, that is nice and glossy and sits in a binder on their shelf – or worse, in the bottom of a drawer. When I first hear a client has an existing business plan, my question is, 'Tell me your values and your vision, mission, or purpose statement'. If you can rattle this off, then you may well have a meaningful document. If you struggle to recall what is in your business plan, then it is simply not serving its purpose.

If you have an existing business plan and you use it as a living, breathing document, then it is valuable and keep using it. The Big Little Business on a Page that we will create will act as a cover sheet to keep your focus razor-sharp. But if you have not opened your business plan for some time and are struggling to recall what is in it, then it is not serving you well and is not adding value to your Little Business. We will create your Big Little Business on a Page that gives you and your team, a visual of who you are and what you do and it will keep you focused on your Big Little Business journey. A simple working document that shapes everything that you do.

VALUES

It all begins with clarifying your personal and business values and understanding why you established your business in the first place. Author Simon Sinek gave an excellent TED Talk titled *How*

Great Leaders Inspire Action. He describes **The Golden Circle**, the WHY, the HOW and the WHAT of business. As he explains, most businesses understand WHAT they do – it might be serving coffee and food, for example. They typically know HOW they do it, by having chefs and baristas prepare quality products for service. However, they often struggle to connect back to the WHY: the core emotion of why they created this business in the first place. And if they have a lack of understanding of their WHY, then so will their team and their clients or customers.

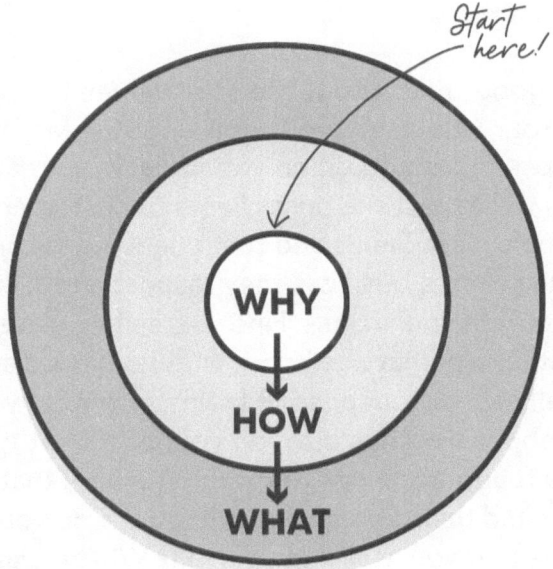

THE GOLDEN CIRCLE

- WHY – this is the core belief of your business, why your business exists
- HOW – the mechanics of how you fulfil your core belief
- WHAT – what you do, your product or service, to meet that core belief

Sinek explains the fundamental difference between the Big Business thinking of the *Apples* of the business world and everyone else, is that they start with WHY. People don't just buy Apple for their products. They buy them for the dream, the vision, the prestige and they are masters of marketing the WHY.

Most businesses start with the WHAT – 'I make great coffee, buy some'. This does not differentiate you from any other coffee shop that sells good coffee. Find your WHY, make the emotional connection and sell me the dream. In straight out marketing terms, sell me the sizzle, not the sausage!

Have a good think about the core values for you in your business. Your values are your non-negotiables. They drive your business focus and guide you in decision-making. Your core values will attract the right clients or customers and also the right employees. Clients and customers like to connect with and purchase from a business they respect and relate to, and this all starts with your values. Find yourself a quiet space with no interruptions (perhaps at home with no work distractions), give yourself half an hour or so to brainstorm what your values are. Think about who has inspired you, and what qualities or actions you found inspiring. Think about a time that you were at your best and think about why. What traits do you admire in other people that you aspire to yourself? What makes you feel good, smile, laugh or feel fulfilled? What actions have you seen in yourself and others that you would like to change, and which would you like to keep the same? Write down your thoughts and answers to these questions, and you will find a theme and some strong values will start coming through.

For me, I was at my best during a time that I was going through rapid business growth. When I look back now, I made some courageous decisions, what some might see as quite risky. I have quite a strong risk profile. However, I mitigate those risks exceptionally well. We had rapid business growth. We built buildings, we bought and sold businesses. And when I look at the traits that allowed me to achieve that, they included a strong focus and attention to detail, a high level of strategic thinking, and a desire to continually improve and to make things better in my business journey. These indeed, are my three core values:

- CONSTANT IMPROVEMENT for lifelong learning
- STRATEGY as the plan for the future
- FOCUS is the way to make it happen

Identify three to five core values that reflect you as a human being, but also your business. Too many values and they won't be meaningful for you so keep it tight. Rather than just single word values, provide behavioural context and understanding as to how those values might be applied to the real world, to your business, your team and your clients or customers.

For example:

- A value of SERVICE might be extended to become *being of SERVICE*
- A value of FUN might become *FUN, but seriously professional*
- A value of RESPECT might become *RESPECTFUL conversations*

PURPOSE

Next on the list is to think about your business purpose. This is something you would have spent quite a bit of time thinking about in the early stages of your business set up, but often it gets lost along the way. Some businesses have a *vision statement*, being a forward-thinking, aspirational statement and also a *mission statement*, being typically a more currently focused statement of intent. Consider replacing these two separate elements with a single *purpose statement*, which defines who you are, what you do and why you do it. This essentially is your position in the marketplace and a strong statement of the intent of your business. Your purpose statement should cover off:

- WHY your business exists
- WHO you serve
- WHAT is the benefit you bring?

Having clarity of your values and your purpose is critical to your business and the first step in creating a solid Big Business strategy. They are who you are and should be front of mind for all of your team and in clear view for your clients or customers to see.

Strong values and a meaningful purpose statement will guide your business decision-making every step of the way. There are many distractions in business. You will find new and shiny opportunities, often presented to you by slick marketers that ultimately serve to meet their goals rather than yours. The once-off opportunity to advertise in a shiny new magazine, *usually $3,999 a month but for the low price of just $999 (per month for 12 months) if you sign up NOW!* Or perhaps a new product is on the market locally that is *taking the rest of the world by storm,* and the sales rep is 'bringing it to you first – but only if you act NOW!'.

Whenever a new opportunity comes forward to you, first assess it based on your values. Is this opportunity consistent with what we have stated? If not, then we don't proceed any further. If it passes the values test, is it also compatible with our purpose statement? If so (and only if so) then we should assess that opportunity and take it on board, if it meets our other assessments.

PILLARS

Beneath our values and purpose statement sit the pillars of our business. The pillars are the core income-generating activities that hold our business up. Ideally, select three to five pillars. Any more than that, and they're just *things we do*, rather than core pillars for our business. Pillars are typically the broad revenue streams that would significantly impact your business if they were no longer there. In other words, if one or two of those pillars were missing, your business would be in trouble. If we take a typical restaurant, for example, that has seated food service as their only offering, then they are a single pillar business, and that is a risk. If that business is unable to open for a period such as we have seen with various disasters, including floods, cyclones, and of course COVID-19, then they are in a world of pain. We have seen single pillar food service businesses close OR adapt and pivot rapidly to extend their offerings in recent times. For example, a seated food service restaurant may now also offer takeaway options, home delivery, or even meal in a box, home cooking options. Some also provide catering to client's homes or workplaces. These new pillars provide diversity to the business and ensure more strength and sustainability.

Once we have identified our key pillars, we *protect and defend* those pillars. Having identified pillars allows us to keep a razor-sharp focus on our essential revenue streams, and we can report on their success or otherwise and take steps to increase their efficiency and profitability. We may, at times, find that two or three of our pillars are strong and one or two are perhaps emerging and/or struggling for a variety of reasons. We need focus to review and strengthen those pillars and this should be discussed in a monthly strategic meeting within your business.

FOUNDATIONS

Sitting beneath the pillars are the all-important foundations, the things that we do, that allow us to deliver on those pillars. This may include your systems and procedures, your customer-focused team, your training processes, your workplace culture, your highly qualified team, your marketing strategy, et cetera. Together, your values, purpose, pillars and foundations form a very simple Big Little Business on a Page that becomes the core of your strategy for your operations.

Developing your Big Little Business on a Page is a time for collaborative leadership. It doesn't have to be perfect. It's a living, breathing document. Get some words on paper, print it out, stick it on the wall where you will see it. Often you will see which words sit well with you and which need to be tweaked. When you're 80% happy with your Big Little Business on a Page, present it to your employees (or trusted friends and family if you are a sole operator) for feedback and workshopping so that the final document is meaningful for your whole team. Typically, others will have a couple of gems that you had not thought about. When your team help to shape your business values and purpose and understand your business pillars and foundations, you can be sure they will work hard to help you achieve that purpose.

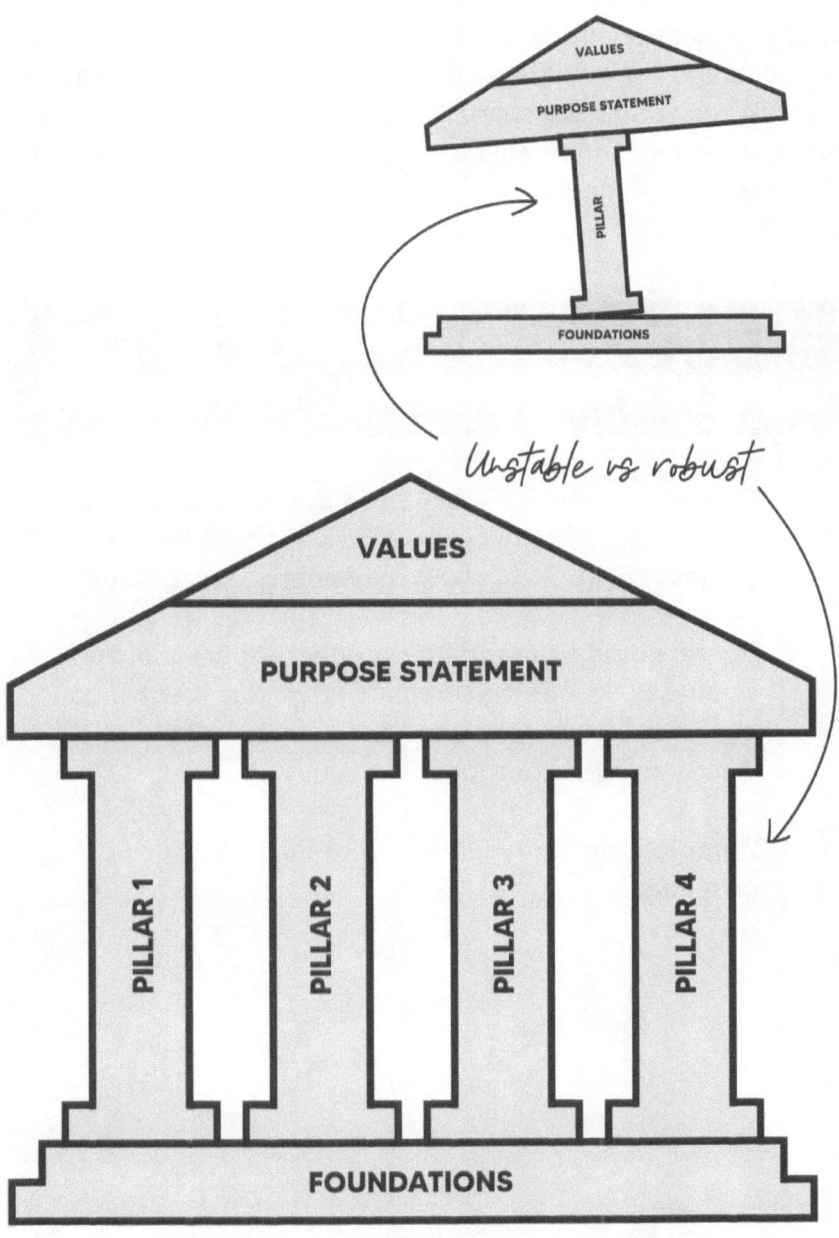

BIG LITTLE BUSINESS ON A PAGE

Your Big Little Business on a Page gives you and your team a clear understanding of your business through your values and purpose and the key areas of your business or pillars that you need to keep that razor sharp focus on. As you progress, you will see that everything relates to and is guided by, your Big Little Business on a Page.

ACTIONS YOU SHOULD TAKE AFTER READING THIS CHAPTER:

1. Download your FREE Big Little Business on a Page workbook to help you develop your own Big Little Business plan. Go to www.jaynearlett.com.au/ebook

2. Spend some time reflecting on your personal and business values to uncover why you went into business in the first place. Find your why. Build your values and your purpose.

3. Complete the framework of your Big Little Business on a Page.

Chapter 2

BIG BUSINESS THINKING

ORGANISATION STRUCTURE

It's hard to be proactive when you're busy being reactive. When you're too busy putting out business bushfires to even think about preventing them. Trust me, I've been there, and I can tell you this proactive versus reactive behaviour is the single biggest differentiator between Big Business and Little Business thinking.

The one thing that turned my Little Business around from struggle street, worrying about people management, being too afraid to look at the bottom line and all the other many things that clog up your brain when you're a business owner, was taking a day a week to work *on* the business, and not *in* the business. I know what you're thinking, 'I don't have the time. I'm way too busy to take a day a week off!' but you're certainly not taking the day off. You're working strategically on the business, putting strategies in place to *prevent those business bushfires*, instead of running around and putting them out, again and again and again.

Working strategically on the business is the key to freeing up your time and giving you the headspace to work on business growth. This is the starting point to systemising and leveraging your business. One of the key things that you will find in Big Business thinking is a solid and clear organisational chart. No matter how Big or how Little your business is, you can benefit from this clarity of structure as well.

A REMINDER FOR MICROBUSINESS AND SOLE TRADERS

You may be thinking your business is too small to need the upcoming C-Suite structure and you simply don't have the people to fill these roles. But the truth is, you already have people doing all these things – and yes, if you are a sole trader, they are all YOU! However, if you are not focused, you will not be doing them well. Segmenting your thought process into each of these roles and putting time in your diary to do so, brings a clear focus, which allows you to perform them all with much better results.

All Little Businesses have the potential to become Big Businesses. And all businesses, Big or Little can function from an organisation chart that looks something like this:

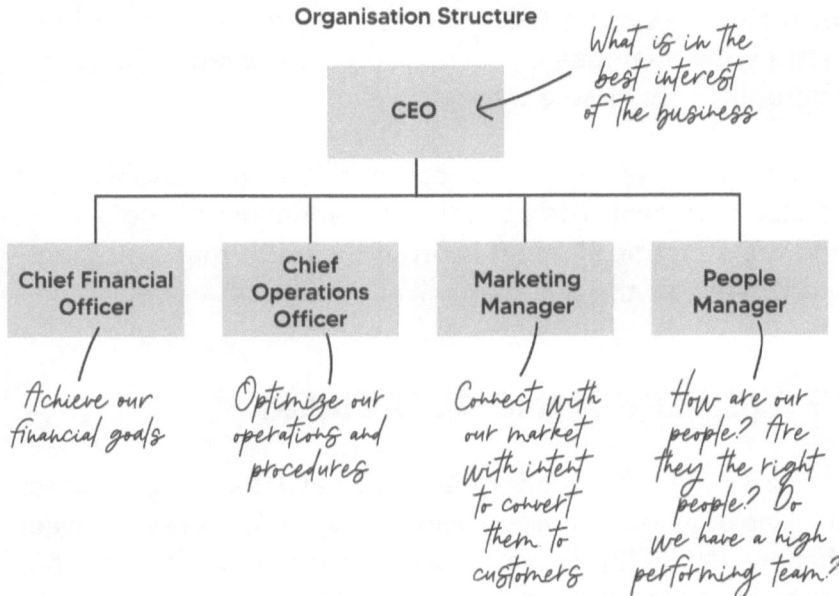

BIG LITTLE BUSINESS ORGANISATION

YOUR METAPHORICAL C-SUITE TEAM

We are going to break the important roles in your Little Business up into their key elements. Now, I'm not saying you need to employ people in each of these roles, it may well be YOU sitting in every one of these positions. But there is an important reason to segment them out – so that you can begin to focus on the elements of business that *make a difference*.

Sitting at the top is the all-important CEO or Chief Executive Officer, the leader of the team. Sitting beneath the CEO are the C-Suite people. You will typically find a CFO (Chief Financial Officer), a COO (Chief Operations Officer), a Marketing Manager, and a People or Human Resources Manager. Larger businesses may have additional C-Suite positions like a Chief Technology, Information, Communication or Green Officer, but essentially, every business can function with these key five C-Suite roles. No matter how Big or Little your business is, you should too, even if you are a microbusiness or sole trader.

Each of these roles has an *operational* element, as well as a *strategic* element. The operational element usually gets done, and the strategic element is often the piece that's missing – but this is also the one that will add the most value!

CFO (CHIEF FINANCIAL OFFICER)

Your CFO is the *money creator*. The CFO in a Big Business thinking organisation will certainly engage in (or have employees that engage in) the **operational** element of the role – they pay the bills, take the money and perform the day-to-day operational element of the finances. But **strategically**, is where they shine, playing a big role in forward-thinking and creating financial opportunities for the business.

As CFO, ask yourself: *How can we achieve our financial goals?* Or quite simply, *How can we make more money?*

COO (CHIEF OPERATIONS OFFICER)

The COO is the *workhorse* of the organisation. This is arguably is the largest role in most businesses – it is what you do on a daily basis. As a business owner, you are likely to be quite an expert at the day-to-day **operations** of what you do and are good at your craft. However, it is the **strategic** element of this role that is most critical to business success.

As COO, ask yourself: *How can I ensure our operations and procedures are optimal? Are they the most efficient? How can we do them better?*

MARKETING MANAGER

Your Marketing Manager is the *rainmaker* and has the power to make or break your business. You cannot sell a secret, but so many Little Businesses waste enormous time and money on ineffective marketing through a lack of understanding and strategic direction. The **operational** element of the Marketing Manager might include scheduling digital and traditional media adverts, creating social media posts, and perhaps arranging sponsorship or an exhibit at an expo to showcase your products.

There is a famous saying in marketing: *I know half of my marketing works; I just don't know which half!* If you are spending a lot of time marketing your business, particularly creating a lot of engaging social media, but it's not driving clients or customers into your door, then what's the point? You must **strategically** look at the ROI (return on investment) for every dollar you spend in your business on marketing, as it can be a big black money pit if it is not used properly.

As Marketing Manager, ask yourself: *How can I best connect to our target market with the intent to convert them to clients or customers?* The important words here being **convert** them to clients or customers.

PEOPLE MANAGER

Your People Manager protects the *human element* of your business, and has a critical job in managing your team, and ensuring everyone functions well – even if your team is only you! This is the most forgotten role for most Little Businesses, but it is recognised as one of the most important in Big Business thinking. **Operationally**, in any business, they will deal with employee crises from time to time, when somebody leaves, or you have multiple people sick, or on holidays at the same time. But very rarely do Little Businesses take the time to think **strategically** about their most valuable resource: their people.

As People Manager, ask yourself: *How are our people? Do I have the correct people, the roles, goals and processes for a high-performing team?*

This is a critical question for all businesses of all sizes, including, (even especially) our microbusinesses and sole traders!

CEO (CHIEF EXECUTIVE OFFICER)

The CEO is the *playmaker* who brings all the elements together. **Operationally**, they are the decision-maker and it is their role to consider all the factors, as well as the upsides and downsides of each issue. If there is a new opportunity on the horizon, they also need to think **strategically** about whether it is consistent with the values and purpose of the business. Does it fit within our existing pillars, or is it a new pillar? Do we have the infrastructure, people and financial resources available? How will we market it and what is the ultimate benefit to the business?

As CEO, ask yourself: *What can I do to make the business better?* And importantly, *What is in the best interest of the business as a whole?*

Take a few minutes now to create your **Big Little Business Organisation Chart** structure and write the names of the responsible people in each of these boxes. If you are a sole operator, it will be your name in each of these C-Suite boxes.

If you have a team of employees, consider carefully if they or you should hold the C-Suite title. Remember each of these roles has an operational element (the easy bit) and a strategic element (the more complex and critical piece). If you have a financial team member who just pays the bills and sends out invoices, they are NOT likely to be the CFO. It may well be your name as the CFO so that you can fulfil the strategic element of this role, with the team member sitting beneath you, fulfilling the operational duties.

If neither you nor a team member has the capacity to fulfil a particular C-Suite role, then consider upskilling yourself as a priority, or outsourcing this element. As a business coach, I work as a parallel CEO, sitting beside the business owner and being another them. We work together on the business as CEO/CFO/COO or any other role as needed. If we have complex marketing needs, for example, we may outsource this to an experienced marketing company to provide the required strategic framework – a review of past marketing activities, a 12-month forward marketing strategy and some training on the operational elements of marketing.

WHAT'S THE POINT?

So, what's the point of separating these roles? It is to separate the function of each of the roles so that you can deeply focus on one element at a time. It's the human tendency to second-guess yourself when you start to think of new ideas. You may have an idea for a new money-making element to your business, but you may be hesitant to move forward with it, because you know you haven't got the right team or the right training, or you're just too busy to put time and energy into growing that new idea right now. So, you cut down the idea before you have even had the chance to explore it fully as a strategy.

But what if you could put on the **metaphorical hat** of a CFO, where your *sole focus* is how to make more money for your business? You can take the time to extend your thought processes fully and evaluate what could be.

One of my favourite strategies is to ask, 'If time, money and skill were no object, how could we do this?'. Once you have that *blue-sky thinking* in place, you will give yourself a chance to explore it before you second-guess it. While not every idea will end up being worthy of implementation, you will at times, come up with fantastic initiatives that are in fact workable and will grow your business.

Similarly, the role of the People Manager is to evaluate how your people are functioning, for example, 'Do we have the right people and systems in place for high performance?'. The strategic element of the People Manager is neglected in so many small businesses. Nothing is reviewed until there is a problem, another people-related business bushfire to put out. But the value in giving yourself forward-thinking strategic planning for your people management will return to you many times over.

It is the role of the CEO to bring it all together, to consider all of the elements of the business. The financial benefit, the operational challenges, how we would market it, and what human resources we need to deliver on this particular idea. The idea of siloing yourself into these different roles is that you really can think strategically about one element without locking it down unnecessarily. The CEO strategic question is always, 'What is in the best interest of the business?'.

Big Business thinking is all about these functions operating, in the initial phases, as silos and asking themselves the *strategic* questions, before the CEO puts it all together.

PUT IT IN YOUR DIARY!

What gets scheduled gets done!

Diary block time each week for your C-Suite people to work on strategy. If it is your name in the relevant boxes, then you schedule this in your diary. If you have a good, strategic team member in this role then they block their time off. I suggest you start with a 30-minute block each week for strategy per role and a one-hour block monthly for your CEO session. You may well increase this time as your business reaps the benefits of this proactive, rather than reactive, thinking.

You don't need to dream up major, ground-breaking initiatives each session. Little improvements, done consistently bring very large benefits to your business. Look for the 'one percenters', the little gains, and do them consistently.

If it is your name in each of these boxes, then schedule two one-hour blocks per week. So, you might have a 30-minute CFO block followed by a 30-minute marketing block on Tuesday mornings with a 30-minute COO block followed by a 30-minute people management block on Thursday afternoons. Monthly, you will schedule a one-hour meeting with yourself as CEO to drill down collectively on each of the elements described below.

- Have a serious meeting with yourself as the CFO on the business financials, metrics and opportunities.
- Understand how the operations of the business are running and can be improved.
- Review your marketing direction and its alignment with the operations of the business (new stock coming in for example). How effective is it? Is it bringing in new business?
- Understand how your people (including you) are functioning and what supports might be needed.

```
┌─────────────────────────────────────────────────────────────┐
│  Date:                              YOUR BUSINESS           │
│  Start time:                         CEO AGENDA             │
│  Attendees:                                                 │
│                                                             │
│  Please bring: C-Suite Reports                              │
├─────────────────────────────────────────────────────────────┤
│  CFO Report      What can I do to achieve our financial     │
│                  goals?                                     │
│                  P&L - report to last year                  │
│                  P&L - report to budget                     │
│                  How are we tracking financially?           │
│                  Financial projects on the horizon          │
├─────────────────────────────────────────────────────────────┤
│  COO Report      How can I ensure our operations and        │
│                  procedures are optimal?                    │
│                  How is the workflow? Where are the         │
│                  bottlenecks?                               │
│                  What are we doing about that?              │
├─────────────────────────────────────────────────────────────┤
│  Marketing       How can I best connect with our target     │
│  Manager         market with the intent to convert them     │
│  Report          to customers?                              │
│                  Where are we at?                           │
│                  Marketing initatives                       │
│                  What's working? What's not? What are we    │
│                  doing about that?                          │
├─────────────────────────────────────────────────────────────┤
│  People          How are our people? Do I have the correct  │
│  Manager         people, roles, goals and process for a     │
│  Report          high performing team?                      │
│                  Team performance - where are we at?        │
│                  New team member - induction/coaching       │
│                  Any other team member needing              │
│                  support/coaching?                          │
├─────────────────────────────────────────────────────────────┤
│  CEO             What can we do to make the business        │
│  Discussion      better?                                    │
│                  Financially                                │
│                  Operationally                              │
│                  Marketing                                  │
│                  People                                     │
│                  What do we need to focus on now?           │
└─────────────────────────────────────────────────────────────┘
```

CEO MEETING AGENDA

When I first started to undertake this level of strategic thinking, I would find myself staring blankly at the wall, wondering what it was I should be thinking about. However, it quickly turned into solid, productive, creative time. It allowed me time to work on building our systems and procedures within the business that created a turnkey (and eminently saleable) business that could work without me. On three occasions I have taken a year out of my business, with minimal involvement through each of those years. Once for overseas postgraduate study, and twice when I had my children (including twins). The business was able to run well with minimal touch points from me due to the structure and processes we had in place, alongside the strong workplace culture we had developed. Taking time out of my week to work consciously and strategically on my business is what allowed me to turn my Little Business into a Big Business.

METAPHORICAL HATS

I have a client that was ready to work strategically on her business, but had a busy, open-plan office. She would get constant interruptions from her team and people walking by her desk. We diary blocked space for her to have her metaphorical time as CFO, COO, Marketing, and People Manager, but she would be constantly interrupted by her team requiring her input to solve today's business bushfires.

She was a keen runner and had a favourite baseball cap. We decided that she would wear her baseball cap at work during the times that she scheduled her strategic sessions. This was a visual signal to her team that she was tuned out from the daily operations of her business, and they knew to not interrupt her through that one-hour block. This allowed her uninterrupted time to focus on the task at hand, and also dramatically improved her team's ability to think for themselves and to develop valuable problem-solving skills. If you do use this type of visual prompt, just remember to remove your hat when the allocated strategic session is over and re-engage with your team!

You are never too small to create an organisation chart. Another of my clients is a fitness instructor, she is a microbusiness and she is the only employee. We created her Big Little Business Organisation Chart and dutifully put her name in each of these boxes. We diary blocked her week, so that she had an hour, twice a week to fulfil one of these blue-sky thinking roles as CFO and Marketing Manager one day, then COO and People Manager, on another. Once a month, she scheduled a meeting with herself as CEO. This time was the time she allowed herself to think things through on that bigger picture scale, factoring in all the required elements.

By then, she had drilled down on what the financial opportunities might be, as well as what operational and people resources (her time) might be required. This allowed her to have a much more complete picture of how things might look, rather than second-guessing and putting up roadblocks for herself before she'd even really had a chance to explore the opportunities. She grew and expanded her business and her offerings including creating a virtual arm to her business, providing online as well as face-to-face fitness training. Even a microbusiness or a sole operator can have enormous benefit from curating a Big Business mindset.

You may still be thinking, I don't know what to do when I have to think strategically. This is about giving yourself space to think. When we are crazy busy working in our businesses, we do not afford ourselves thinking time. It takes a while to get into a strategic headspace. Give yourself time to ponder the strategic questions, as CFO for example, 'How do I make more money?'. After a few sessions, you'll be strategising like a pro.

ACTIONS YOU SHOULD TAKE AFTER READING THIS CHAPTER:

1. Create your own Big Little Business Organisation chart, putting your name, or the name of your team members, in each of the areas.

2. Diary block time in your schedule for strategic thinking under each of these hats. A 60-minute block, twice a week is a great start, plus a once a month 60-minute session as CEO.

3. Find yourself a hat or come up with some other metaphorical prompt to put you in the mindset of each role as you put it on – and to notify your team that you are 'off limits'!

Chapter 3

BUT ARE YOU REALLY MAKING MONEY?

REVENUE IS VANITY, PROFIT IS REALITY

'I thought my business needed to be profitable before I could engage a business coach – but now I realise I needed a business coach so my business could become profitable!'

This comment came from one of my lovely coaching clients in just the third week of us working together. She had a large, well-established service business with a high profile and a turnover to match. It's a complex business with many revenue elements and a team in excess of 60 (including regular contract professionals). From the outside looking in, it looks like a highly successful business – but she was drawing a personal wage that was barely that of her most junior team member and was highly anxious each month to see if they had covered their costs. She just could not understand where all the money was going.

When I asked her, what was the most profitable part of her business, she said, 'That's easy,' and gave me her answer. When I asked her, what was the net profit percentage of that element of her business, she had no idea. What she was focused on was the turnover, not the profit.

This was a service element of her business, delivered by contract professionals who were paid a percentage of their billings. She understood the gross profit – the revenue less the hard costs of the professional contract team who deliver this service – and the gross profit was nicely positive, meaning her revenue was more than her direct costs. But she had not drilled down to factor in all the other costs of her support team, infrastructure costs, consumable costs and the significant portion of rent that this particular element of the business required. This element was responsible for over 50% of the turnover revenue of the business. But when we drilled down into the REAL costs associated with running that element, she was barely breaking even! Each client she saw was almost *costing* her money.

We detailed the real costs of delivering this service and very quickly put a strategy in place to turn this situation around. This included increasing her fee for the service, but also adjusting the contractor percentage down to allow her to adequately cover the real costs of delivering this service. This was done strategically, at the same time. The contractor percentage return decreased, but the billing amount increased sufficiently so the payment the contractors received per service also increased. But importantly, the margin available to the business increased significantly, strengthening the bottom line, building a sustainable business and allowing the business owner to sleep at night!

Like many businesses, this owner was very hesitant, overly so, about increasing her prices, being concerned about her customer reaction to a price hike. However, this was a high-profile business with an established and loyal customer base and a strong reputation in the region. After some market and competitor research, we were comfortable the increase would be accepted by our customers, which it was. This one small change that we made, within two weeks of working together, made an annualised increase to her bottom line of $50,000.

PROFIT CENTRES

Business is hard work. Many people try to run a business, and sadly many people fail. The Australian Bureau of Statistics, reports that, in 2019, there were almost 2.4 million active businesses in Australia, but in that same year, almost 300,000 businesses closed their doors. Make sure you understand the difference between revenue, gross profit and net profit – and, even more importantly, that you understand which levers to pull in your business to increase that net profit. This is the key to success, and it can be the difference between thriving or becoming one of those 300,000 businesses that have to exit the market.

Let's go back and look at those pillars that we set up in our Big Little Business on a Page. These are the key revenue areas of your business and we must protect and defend them. It's critical that we break down each element of those pillars correctly and identify the profit centres.

To do this, we first need to factor in the hard cost, the direct cost of the service or goods, for example, the cost of the contractor in the scenario above, the cost of food for a restaurant or the cost of an item of clothing for a fashion retailer. This is generally called Cost of Goods Sold (or COGS) and this is what most business owners are largely focused on. However, there is a critical next step, that is so often overlooked – that is, factoring the myriad of other costs that apply to operating your business into each item or service that you sell.

Who pays for your rent, your insurance, your employee's time to pack and unpack your products? Who pays for the electricity, the telephone, et cetera? The answer is, **you do!** And unless you factor that into the cost of your product or service, it comes straight off your bottom line, out of your profit. So, make sure that you look at each element of the business revenue and calculate the *true* costs, not just the obvious hard costs associated with running that service or buying that product.

Time and time again, I have walked into a new client's business and see that they have an enormous, well-appointed, office that looks impressive but is simply not being used well. They forget that that space *owes them money.* If you have a vacant room or two, or an underutilised space, the rent you pay for that space is a hard cost that comes out of your bottom line. If you have a service, such as a medical practice using consulting rooms or a beauty service business, you must factor in the cost of those rooms for the treatments that are used. This can be as simple as taking your average monthly business expenses from your P&L and dividing it by the average number of customers per month.

CALCULATING YOUR REAL COSTS

It's not uncommon when we drill down on each area of business revenue to this level, that we find that there are several elements of business products or services that a business offers that are barely breaking even. In fact, on occasions, we find that some are actually costing the business – meaning every time they deliver that service or product they *lose* money.

At times, we may choose to offer what we call a *loss leader* product or service, something that we know we are going to take a hit on and lose money. That is acceptable if it brings you some other benefit in return, in this case we would consider it a part of our marketing strategy. For example, a common loss leader is a supermarket that might sell a loaf of bread for a dollar or two. It costs them more than that to produce that loaf of bread, so they lose money for every loaf that they sell. But very rarely will somebody walk into a supermarket and walk out with just that one item. CHOICE research tells us the average spend per supermarket shop in Australia is around $100. So, the loss leader is the cheap bread to attract the customer in, and the benefit to the business is the profit on the remainder of the $100 spend.

The important thing about analysing your profit centres to this level is that you truly understand which are the loss leaders in your business, as you can then assess if they are of value to you. So, if the business is losing $10 or $20 each time you offer a particular service or product, is there enough additional revenue that comes in from introducing that client or customer to your business to make it worthwhile? If not, we need to rethink our pricing strategy or delete that service or product altogether.

Similarly, understanding the profitability of each element is critical when you're going through a growth bubble. I have a client in a large, service business who was experiencing very rapid growth but had difficulty acquiring the required specialist employees to manage the influx of work. He had a significant waiting list and the business was bursting at the seams with referrals. We analysed the profit centres of each market segment of the clients that came through the doors and we identified the high profitability versus the low profitability client segments. This gave us the power to strategically pick and choose which elements of the business we would continue with and which we would *pause* until we could secure additional employees. This is a good example of high-level strategic decision-making that allowed this business to make a call about which areas needed to be serviced at the usual high level and which areas we could comfortably hold off for a period.

CRUNCHING THE NUMBERS

Please don't be frightened of the numbers in your business. So many people tell themselves that they are no good with numbers and they don't enjoy the money side of the business. After all, for most people (unless you are a bookkeeper or an accountant), you didn't go into business to look at the numbers all day. You went into business to do the things that you enjoy, the things that you are good at, the areas of your technical skill. However, ignoring the numbers is what can lead, time and time again, to business failure. In Chapter Four: **The Financial Detective**, we will drill down into the numbers in a lot more detail and I will help you to become the Financial Detective of your own business!

When we look at the profit centres of your business, these are the different elements that earn you revenue. In a coffee shop, for example, you might have three pillars:

- meals that are served in-house
- takeaway coffee and food
- external catering

You might receive the greatest revenue from your catering pillar, but it's important to understand the profitability once you factor in all the associated costs. This includes the cost of goods (your food and product costs) but also allocating a portion of the other business costs, such as rent, utilities, wages and in the catering segment, the cost of delivery which might include a vehicle and specialised equipment to keep food hot or cold, plus the additional time for a team member to make the delivery. In this example, you would factor in COGS and all business expenses for the takeaway and in-house service pillars, and these costs *plus* the additional costs of the vehicle and specialised equipment for the catering pillar. This allows us to ensure each element of the business is turning a profit.

Let's crunch the numbers for a clothing retail outlet that has the following figures:

- $180 is the average spend per customer
- 250 customers are served on average, per month
- 50% GP (gross profit margin) or a 100% mark-up on product cost

So, the $180 average spend on clothing costs the store $90 for the cost of goods sold or COGS. The remaining $90 gross profit or GP needs to now have the business costs factored in before we can understand the bottom line.

The simplest way to do this for this business is to take the average rent, wages and all other business costs for the month and divide by the average number of sales or customers in this instance. This business has a monthly running cost of $18,500. Divide this by the 250 customers it sees each month and each sale has to contribute $74 out of the $90 gross profit. The net profit then is $16 ($90 - $74) or 9% of the original sale price.

Rent, wages and other business costs

Operation costs/month	$
Total Monthly Cost	18,500.00
Sales per month	250
Business Cost Per Sale	74.00

Increase average spend increases profits!

Current position

Profit centre	$	$	$
Average Sale	180.00	200.00	220.00
Cost of Goods	90.00	100.00	110.00
Gross Profit	90.00	100.00	110.00
Business Cost Per Sale	74.00	74.00	74.00
Net Profit Per Sale	16.00	26.00	36.00
Net Profit Per Sale (250 sales)	9%	13%	16%

PROFIT CENTRE CALCULATION

You can see that this business has a 50% gross profit and a 9% net profit on the bottom line based on its current situation of a $180 average sale. Having this calculation now allows us to run various scenarios like increasing our average sale from $180 to $200 or $220. This will increase the net profit from 9% to 13% or 16% respectively. Similarly, if you reduce your costs or increase the number of customers per month this will make a significant difference to your bottom line.

If you've never undertaken profit centre analysis before, please don't feel alone. Most Little Businesses don't, which is one of the reasons that so many of them struggle to grow. I see them every day running their businesses and kicking along – just not as well as they could with a little more understanding. Business, like life, is a journey. Lack of understanding does not mean the end of the journey, but life and business become easier and more enjoyable as we learn and progress.

Understanding the back end of your business is the key to success. It gives you immense power over your business. You now control it. The business does not control you! Understanding the money and your profit centres is about you taking charge and steering your business the way that you want to go.

OWNER'S WAGES – DIRECTOR'S DRAWINGS

I am often asked if the wages or drawings for the business owner should be factored into these business calculations or just the 'staff' wages. My answer is, 'Only if you want to get paid'. This is very tongue in cheek – the real answer is a very loud YES! It breaks my heart to see so many businesses, being run by owners that are not being paid a fair wage themselves. One of the greatest myths about business is that all business owners are 'rich'! Whilst certainly some business owners do very well, many Little Business owners struggle. Some have essentially *bought themselves a job* rather than a business and barely make a living wage – and some (like me in the early years) work for nothing! That is acceptable if it is short term and part of a bigger plan, but I work very hard with businesses to develop a financially sustainable business and provide a decent wage to the business owner as soon as possible. So yes! Factor in your own wage into any financial calculations with the same priority that you factor in your employees' wages.

OPPORTUNITY COST

A quick word here to keep an eye on the opportunity costs within your business. In the early stages of business, the owner will perform most of the operational tasks – you have time on your hands and there is often no money to pay anyone else! This might mean you do the bookwork, administration duties and even the office cleaning. As your Little Business grows and the demands on your time increase, consider the opportunity cost of you continuing with these duties as compared to outsourcing this task. What value would you bring to the business if you did not do these tasks?

Let's say you spend five hours a week managing your books. If you outsourced this to a bookkeeper at a cost of $1,000 monthly, this frees up around 20 hours each month of your time. What's the opportunity for your business here? What could you do with an extra 20 hours a month? If you put this time into your business in another way – selling your product or service, or working strategically in growing the business, do you have the opportunity to earn the business more than $1,000? If so, the opportunity cost for you to be doing your bookwork may be too great.

ACTIONS YOU SHOULD TAKE AFTER READING THIS CHAPTER:

1. Think about which elements of your business bring in the most revenue. These will be within the pillars in your Big Little Business on a Page.

2. Cost out *everything* associated with the delivery of each product and service and calculate your net profit per element.

3. Prioritise your sales and marketing based around the most important profit centres for you.

Chapter 4

THE FINANCIAL DETECTIVE

SHOW ME THE NUMBERS!

Call me strange, but I love numbers. Show me the numbers of your business, your profit and loss, your KPIs, your balance sheet, and I can tell you a lot about your business, possibly more than you already know. Show me the numbers, because that is where the *truth* lies.

Now I understand that not everybody wants to be a financial guru. That's not why you went into business and you don't have to learn to be an accountant to run your business. But what you should be, is confident enough to look at your financials bravely, and understand enough to know when your business is going well, and when you need to seek help.

Learning about the financials of your business is like riding a bike or driving a car. It's incredibly complex and confusing when you first do it! If you've ever had to teach a teenager how to drive, you will understand how many processes there are that you, as an experienced driver, now do on autopilot. It's the same with understanding the financials of your business. What looks complex and foreign right now will become second nature with time. So read on, to find the Financial Detective within you!

If you don't feel you have a good handle on your financials, you are certainly not alone. A study on financial literacy and the success of small business from the University of South Florida showed that 50% of businesses do **not** regularly review their financial statements, and of those, 85% experienced financial difficulties. Conversely, of the businesses that do regularly review their financial statements, just 14% of them experienced financial difficulties. Not surprisingly, the strong message here is that financial awareness is key to financial success. You can't reverse a problem that you don't even know that you have.

By the time we've finished this chapter, you will not be frightened to read your financial documents. You will understand the five key financial documents of your business and how to use them to control and drive your business forward. Heck, you might even be excited to receive your P&L from your bookkeeper and look forward to reading it.

THE BIG FIVE

So, let's look at five key financial documents that should be part of every small business financial arsenal.

1. **Your Profit and Loss (P&L), also known as an Income Statement.** The income is at the top, the expenses are

underneath. Below this, the bottom line or net profit is the difference between the two – and we need it to be a positive number! P&Ls serve two purposes in business: one is for your accountant and your end of financial year tax planning and the second is to be a useful and practical financial management tool for you to use now. Understand your P&L inside out and use it as an active part of your business management.

2. **The Magic Budget**. A budget, combined with your P&L is singly, the most important document you should have in your financial arsenal. It's also the one most Little Businesses don't use. I call all budgets *the magic budget* as they are so powerful. More to come on this topic.
3. **A KPI Dashboard**. Key performance indicators are accountability measures for your business and your team. These are the key metrics that make a difference in your business and are indicators of success. You should watch them closely.
4. **Cash Flow Forecast**. This is an enormously helpful document when you're in a crisis situation or just a bit of a tight spot. In fact, it's more than helpful, it's critical. Get used to using cash flows. They'll save your skin one day.
5. **The Balance Sheet, also known as your Statement of Financial Position**. The balance sheet is simply a summary of all the business assets and liabilities – in short, what the business owns and what it owes at any particular point in time. It shows you what would be left over if you sold all your assets and paid off all your debts, otherwise known as the owner's equity or the business net worth.

CFO – YOUR TIME TO SHINE!

The real value I add in working with small businesses is teaching them to be their own Financial Detective, to get comfortable wearing their metaphorical CFO hat, and to understand their financials. This is like having a regular check-up at the doctor. It helps you understand the health (or otherwise) of your business. What's working, what's not, and most importantly, what you can do about it.

So, what does this all mean for your Little Business and how will it help you grow? Little Business thinking is to receive the financial reports monthly, print them off and put them in a folder. Many Little Businesses will quickly scan through the P&Ls, have a look at the bottom line, be pleased or frightened by the result, and then put it away until next month. Big Business thinking is to pour over the P&Ls with their CFO hat on, compare them carefully to the budget, and to analyse what's happened – with the intent to capitalise on the good and to mitigate and correct the bad.

Little Business response upon reviewing their P&Ls in a good month will be a relief and, 'We had a good month. That's great,' then move on. In a bad month, it will be shock, disappointment, worry and fear.

Big Business strategy is to engage their CFO thought process while reviewing their P&Ls. In a good month, their response is, 'We had a good month. That's great! How did we do that? How can we do more of that?' In a bad month, there will again be a strategic thought process, 'How did that happen? What are we going to do about that?' And importantly, 'What will we do to make up the deficit?'.

Big Business thinking will always be to understand *why* the business had the result it did. To identify the levers it can pull to maximise the good result and minimise the bad. Always remember, if you make a profit in a particular month, the extra money goes straight to your bottom line. You can use this to reinvest back into your business, or when things are going well, it can go into the business owner's pocket as drawings. If you make a loss, that will be a deficit on your bottom line, and that ultimately comes directly out of the business owner's pocket. If you don't rectify that deficit and if the trend continues, your business will eventually fold.

THE MAGIC BUDGET

Working with a budget is where the magic happens in business. Most Little Businesses don't operate on a budget, but once you start using one effectively, it will change your world.

The absence of a budget is one of the critical differences between a Big Business and Little Business mindset. There are no large businesses that would dream of operating without a budget (and sticking to it), whereas most small businesses simply never set one up.

One client of mine was a typical Little Business. She had been established for many years and had a good little team. She was turning over around $500k, not too shabby but there was no strategy, no growth and no budget! Worse still, she was drawing a minimal wage, less than most of her employees and there was barely any profit on the bottom line. She told me she didn't understand the money side of the business and would quickly scan her P&Ls before filing them away in a nice folder. She only understood her financial situation once a year, when her accountant told her how she had done – retrospectively, after it was too late to change anything!

The first year we worked together we set a growth strategy and an ambitious goal of 20% revenue increase with a profitable bottom line. We worked to find her inner Financial Detective and importantly we created a magic budget with that 20% revenue uplift. She set her mind to achieve this figure and she and her team explored opportunities and worked hard on the growth strategies we had set. She hit the budgeted 20% uplift for the first month, in the second month she exceeded the magic budget and was around 30% up, and she began to get excited to check the figures each month. We would report the P&L to budget and with her CFO hat on, she would pour over the variances, drilling down on the exceptions. Seeking to understand *how* she had exceeded her budget and how she could do more of that, as well as picking up on any overspends in the expenses section. We had a major blow out in her marketing budget one month, so she simply reduced her spend in subsequent months. Tightening her belt and taking from the future allocations in other areas to cover overspending allowed her to balance the books – without affecting her bottom line. By the end of that first year, she had smacked that 20% goal out of the water and had achieved a massive 50% increase in revenue! As she also now had tight control over the expenses, her bottom-line profit had more than tripled which allowed her to draw a decent income for the first time as a business owner. The magic budget had done its job.

YOUR FIRST MAGIC BUDGET

Setting up your budget for the first time is not as difficult as you might think. The first year you run a budget will certainly be a learning period, but it will add so much value that you will look forward to looking at it each month. Having a budget fosters a strong growth mindset – you have set yourself a clear goal for the month and you will be inclined to work to achieve it!

To get started, print out your P&Ls for the last three financial years (or for as long as you have if you are a new business). Businesses change over the years of course but you will see where the trends are. Have a look at your income or your gross revenue and project forward where you think you might be for the upcoming year. In a tough market, you might be pleased to have a very modest increase of a couple of per cent, but if you're on a growth trajectory, then don't be afraid to put in 15, 20, even 30%, depending on your particular business and opportunities.

Income targets, like most goals in life, should be achievable, but with a little stretch. Have a look at whether your revenue is chunky or consistent. Is it seasonal? Are you busy in December or is that a flat time for you? Vary your expected revenue per month if you have regular trends, or simply divide your projected annual income by 12 to get started. Put that number in the budget section of your financial management software. The expenses are usually much easier to budget, particularly if you've been in business for a couple of years, as you will be able to see from your P&Ls quite clearly how much money you've spent on marketing, accountancy fees, rent, utilities, office supplies, IT, motor vehicles, et cetera. Some of these things like electricity, insurance or various fees or memberships, you may pay quarterly or annually, so place that expense in the appropriate month. Most other expenses can be divided by 12 so you have equal allocations per month. Marketing may be chunky, if you run major promotions based around seasonal flows or various expos or activities to market your business. Divide your annual budgeted spend into the months that you anticipate this spend will occur, otherwise, again, you can divide by 12 for equal monthly allocations.

Once you have set your budget, we then report monthly with your actual figures, comparing your P&Ls to your budget. Most financial management software will create that comparison as an automatic function. What we are doing is reporting by exception. So, if you have set your expenses correctly, you should have a variance of no more than 5% either way. If you have a large variance, then put your CFO hat on again and analyse *why* and adjust. For example, if you spend more on your marketing than you had budgeted this month, *what are you going to do about that?* If this increased marketing spend hasn't realised a corresponding increase in revenue, then you will have to pinch from your future marketing spend to not impact negatively on your bottom line. Please don't ignore any failure to hit your revenue targets or any overspend in your expenses because any variance here will come straight from your pocket as the business owner.

Whether you have had a good and profitable month or a difficult one with a loss, be your own Financial Detective and ask yourself the strategic questions so you can do more of the things that bring you profit and less of the things that cause the loss.

KPI DASHBOARD

The KPI dashboard is a much-overlooked financial tool, and one that is well worth setting up in your business. Have a look at your Big Little Business on a Page and the key pillars of your business. What are the key indicators of your business that will drive its profitability? Set your KPI benchmarks and these become the goals for your team to help you achieve.

We talk here about two separate indicators, a lead indicator, and a lag indicator. Most businesses work on lag indicators, which are historical data that's already happened and cannot be changed. A classic example of a lag indicator is your profit and loss statement for last month. It's already happened, and you can't change that now.

A lead indicator though, is a predictor of likely future income. It might be the number of new listings that a real estate agent secures each month because we know the more listings we have, the more revenue we can generate as we convert these to sales. New client enquiries can be a lead indicator for a car dealership if we know we will convert a certain percentage to a sale, and forward bookings for tourism operators are another example that gives us an indication of future revenue. For many service-based businesses, we look at new clients or customers that we service each month. We know that at times, existing clients or customers will move on. They may no longer require the product or service you offer, physically move location, or they may choose to try another business. So, if you don't have a ready stream of new clients or customers coming in, eventually your business will run into trouble.

Another classic dashboard metric is wages, which is a major cost for the majority of businesses, reported as a percentage of revenue or a ratio. For each business, it will be different, but if you track your business trends, you will see what multiple you need from your employees' wages to your revenue to be a profitable business. It might be a 3:1 ratio where you need your wages to sit at no more than 33% of revenue, or a 1:1 ratio where a 50% wage cost is acceptable. Every industry and every business is different, but keeping a close eye on your wages spend is important for all businesses.

Think about key indicators or key metrics that are useful for your particular business and see how you can put that into a graph form on a dashboard page so that each month you can produce a clear vision as to what your financial position is.

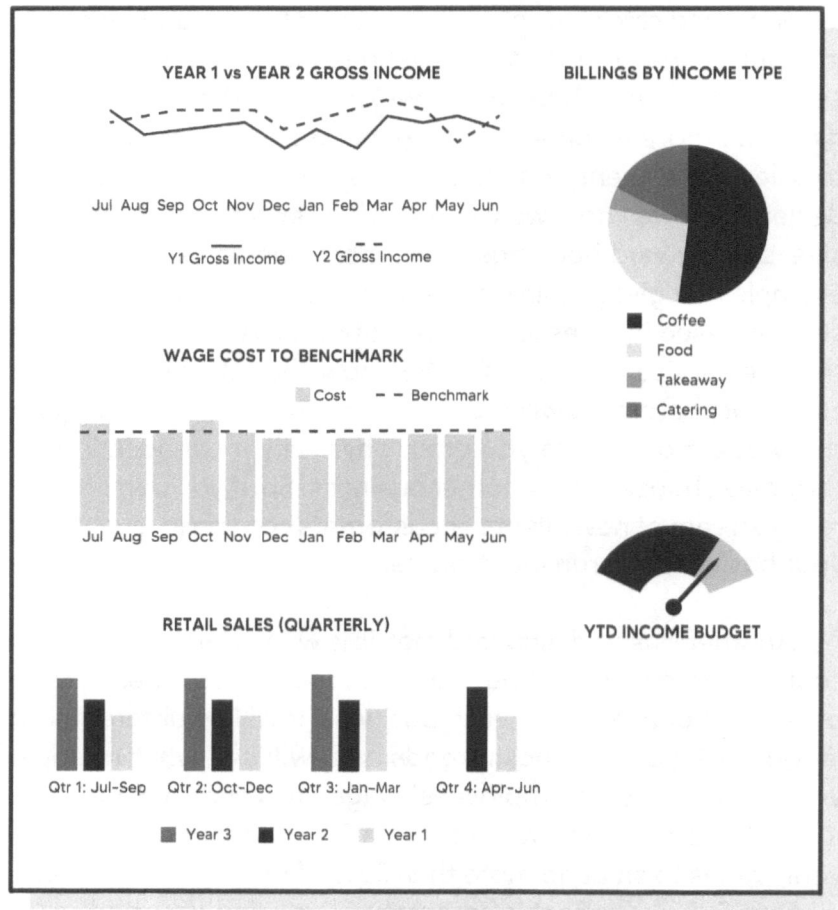

KPI DASHBOARD

CASH FLOW FORECAST

The next financial document we're going to look at is a cash flow document. And again, most small businesses don't do this. In fact, most small businesses will manage by how much cash they have in the bank. Please don't do this! It's not real, this does not allow for upcoming bills. You need to manage by your financial documents and by understanding what bills are due and payable in the upcoming weeks and months. Your P&L and your magic budget are the best ways to manage your business.

A cash flow forecast can also be very helpful. Most financial management software packages will have these available to you. However, it's a very simple exercise to set up a 12-week or a 12-month cash flow forecast in Excel. Simply start with your opening bank balance in the top line, followed by your total expected revenue in, and then your total expected expenses out (you can find this in your magic budget). This will give you your closing bank balance at the bottom, which automatically transfers up to the top line for the following week or month. When you do this for multiple weeks or months in advance, you can predict what your cash flow will be and based on the budgeting that you have just done, you can see for example, that you may run into cash flow trouble in several months down the track if you predict your revenue will decrease during the slow time of the year. This allows you to curtail your spending, to do a concerted marketing push to increase your revenue to prevent this from occurring, or arrange an overdraft to see you through that period, if you know it's a short-term cash flow problem.

Complete for the whole year →

YOUR BUSINESS	September	October	November
Opening Bank Balance	$20,000	$23,000	$19,500
Plus Total Cash in	$44,000	$38,000	$47,500
Less Total Cash out	$41,000	$41,500	$42,000
Closing Bank Balance	$23,000	$19,500	$25,000

Closing balance becomes next months opening balance

CASH FLOW FORECAST

BALANCE SHEET/STATEMENT OF FINANCIAL POSITION

The balance sheet, as a general rule, doesn't change dramatically very often, but you should be aware of current assets and liabilities vs. fixed assets and liabilities. The word *current* on your balance sheet means 12 months. So, a current asset is something that you can turn to cash (or liquidate) in a short period. Your current assets might include your cash in the bank, short-term investments that you may have, the stock that you can sell and debtors or people that owe you money.

The main thing that you should be concerned with in your balance sheet is that your current assets are greater than your current liabilities. That is called a solvency test and means that you have sufficient assets to cover your liabilities, that you can pay your bills when they fall payable. The balance sheet shows your owner's equity or business net worth. Work on growing the bottom line on your balance sheet each year – reducing your liabilities and increasing your assets.

Balance sheets are important documents and you should review them regularly, but there is not too much else to worry about on your balance sheet. It doesn't change rapidly and provided your assets are greater than your liabilities (in particular that your current assets exceed your current liabilities), then you can sleep well at night.

TAX

Shall I be controversial and say paying tax is a good thing?

Now I don't for one minute want you to pay any more tax than you need to, but at times I see business owners doing things to reduce their tax that are to the *detriment* of their business – buying equipment that they don't need, replacing items that are still perfectly functional. I have even seen businesses actively stop earning money, turning away revenue because they don't want to pay tax on it!

Run your business consistently with your values and purpose. Focus on those pillars, understand your profit centres. Capitalise on the areas that make you money and minimise the ones that don't. Work closely with an accountant that understands your business and your purpose. You should be running a profitable business and you will pay tax on that. By all means engage in tax minimising strategies, but reducing tax should never be the primary driver of any new purchase; achieving your business goals should.

YOUR FIRST MILLION IS THE HARDEST TO MAKE

Finally, with financials, understand the economies of scale. One of my favourite sayings in business is *your first million is the hardest to make*. A million-dollar revenue is a tipping point for many Little Businesses. It's a hard slog to pay the rent, utilities, insurances and fixed costs of any small business. And typically, many of these costs are very similar whether you earn under a million or over a million. So a business with a $200,000–$500,000 turnover has similar fixed costs as the same business with a $1 million turnover, and yet the profitability will skyrocket once you hit over that magic million as those costs are already paid for.

I have a client in a volatile industry, their revenue per client can be significant but it's sporadic. They had been in business for about 10 years but were just not getting ahead. We worked as Financial Detectives to analyse the past trends and it was clear that they were hovering around the million-dollar annual revenue mark each year. Every time they tipped over the million dollars in revenue, their bottom line was healthy and the years they just couldn't make it to the million, they struggled to break even. It was clear they had to make a million as their baseline to cover their costs comfortably. We set up a budget and some targets. We employed an additional revenue earning team member and put them and the rest of the team to work with some clear KPI's.

They achieved that million-dollar revenue the very first year and we have a pact that they will never drop below a million again. Now they have their magic budget in place, and they are their own Financial Detectives controlling their business, I think it won't be too long before they top $2 million. So do the hard yards in your business, do it quickly, get your revenue up to that magic $1 million, and let's watch you fly.

ACTIONS YOU SHOULD TAKE AFTER READING THIS CHAPTER:

1. Understand how to read your financial documents and do this monthly, with your CFO hat on.

2. Set your business a magic budget for the year, no matter what stage of the annual financial cycle we are in when you read this, and then report your P&Ls to your budget monthly.

3. Understand the key lead indicators for your business and how to control them.

4. Explore your financial management software (or use Excel) and have a play with creating a cash flow forecast.

Chapter 5
I SEE YOU!

YOU CAN'T SELL A SECRET

Marketing is the *rainmaker* of your business. It will make or break you.

You may have the best product or service in the world, but if no-one knows about it, your dream Little Business will fail. The trick is to understand your market and make every marketing dollar count.

Most businesses have a good idea of who their current clients or customers are – but are they the best fit for your business? Let's face it, some people are just difficult to deal with and the old line *the customer is always right* is most certainly not true. Spending some time thinking about your ideal clients or customers rather than your actual clients or customers, can make a significant difference in how you do business, your level of profitability and your individual satisfaction. Having your business full of ideal clients or customers will make life so much easier for you.

So, put on your metaphorical marketing manager hat and let's consider what your ideal customer might look like. For most businesses, there are five elements of an ideal client or customer behaviour:

- they pay on time
- they accept your fees, or if they do question them, they do so respectfully
- they value your product or service
- they refer other clients or customers
- they share your values

So, what does this look like for your Little Business? Well, if you are a cafe, it might mean that your ideal customers don't complain about the cost of your coffee. They love your offerings and they compliment you. They bring friends in at times to share a coffee and a meal with them and importantly for the growth of your Little Business, they positively review and share your business on socials. Last but not least, they share your values so you will like them, and they will like you. Fundamentally, this makes them great customers to have.

What does this mean if you're a law firm or an accountant? It means you don't have to chase your clients for payments. They will accept your fees or question them respectfully. They will value your advice and act upon it. They bring other work to your firm and they refer friends and family. Again, they share your values so you will like them, and they will like you.

AVATARS

An avatar is a little bit of fiction that helps us understand our ideal clients – to SEE them. We humanise and personalise our ideal client avatars so that we can gain a strong understanding of them. This gives us valuable insights into where we can find them and how we can market to them effectively. Avatars are detailed profiles of each of your ideal customer segments. They go into greater depths than traditional marketing personas, which allows us to apply more effective, targeted marketing.

Have a look at the key pillars of your business. What are your main revenue streams? You may well have different ideal clients for each pillar. Let's personalise an avatar for each. Create an avatar for your ideal clients, a single page for each, where you build a profile of what that client would look like.

So, for example, if we own a cafe and we are aiming at an upmarket corporate customer base, we might create an avatar that we will call Mary. We need to understand who Mary is, so we might create a general description of:

- Age: 40 to 60 years
- Gender: female
- Domestic situation: partnered with older or adult children, perhaps an empty-nester
- Residence: likely to own her own home, possibly inner city
- Occupation: a professional, perhaps a manager
- Income: $70K plus, she has a reasonably high disposable income
- Activities: social media, she's likely to exercise with friends, she may well be creative and appreciate good design. And she will, of course, frequent coffee shops and perhaps art galleries

We will then break this up into the four key elements that describe Mary's behaviour.

1. Her goals and values.
- We might assume that Mary has a wide circle of friends and likes to exercise with them and catch-up in cafes.
- She values quality service. She appreciates stylish decor and art.
- She sometimes brings work or has regular meetings at her 'coffice', so she needs a pleasant space that is suitable for both social and work catch-ups.

2. Where does she hang out?
- Mary is likely to be active on social media, particularly Facebook and Instagram.
- She may well be a regular at a gym and/or boot camps.
- She attends business networking events.
- She may be part of art groups or book clubs and frequent mid to high-end restaurants.

3. Her wants and needs, or her pain points.
- She's an empty-nester. She enjoys social contact.
- She expects quality products and services in a stylish and comfortable environment.
- When at a cafe there may be times that she wants to be visible and highly social and other times she may need some privacy when she is having a work meeting.

4. How do we help? The gain points we offer.
- We provide an upmarket cafe on trend, but not too trendy.
- We have beautiful decor and provide a comfortable environment with seating areas that are both suited to social and casual work catch-ups.
- Our team are friendly and greet regular customers by name.
- We are Mary's go-to 'coffice' and social hangout.

We will personalise Mary's avatar with a photo. We may well build Mary's avatar based around an existing ideal client or take a combination of clients and turn them into one ideal. The secret here is to personalise the avatar to the level that we have just done so that you can really understand what your ideal customer is like – and very, very importantly, know where they hang out. Once we understand that somebody like Mary is likely to be active on social media, and in particular Facebook and Instagram, then we can target our marketing directly to that. Similarly, if she's likely to be fitness-oriented then we can target our advertising towards gyms and boot camps. We know that she's likely to hang out at business networking groups so we can choose to strategically network with women in that social circle or sponsor business events.

Drilling down on an avatar to this level means that we can target our marketing and get the best bang for our marketing buck. Similarly, understanding what her wants and needs are, her *pain points*, allows us to tweak our offering to best suit our ideal client. Not everybody wants to be on show and in an open social environment all the time. If she's likely to want to have work meetings in our cafe, then we must provide little nooks and crannies where she can meet more privately.

MY CAFE Ideal Client/ Customer Avatar  **Mary** Age: 40-60 Domestic: partnered, adult child(ren) Location: own home, inner city Occupation: Manager Annual Income: $70k+ Education: Tertiary Other: active on socials; exercises with friends; appreciates good design; frequents coffee shops and galleries	**GOALS & VALUES** ✓ Mary has a wide circle of friends and likes to exercise with them and catch up in cafés ✓ She has a reasonably high disposable income, values quality, service and appreciates stylish décor ✓ She sometimes brings work or has meetings at her regular 'coffice'	**ENGAGE** ✓ Mary is active on social media, FB and Instagram ✓ She is a regular at her gym/bootcamps ✓ She attends business networking groups ✓ Art groups/book clubs ✓ Mid/high end restaurants
	WANTS & NEEDS (PAIN POINTS) ✓ Enjoys social contact ✓ Wants quality product and service ✓ Wants a stylish and comfortable environment ✓ When at café - might want to be visible (social) or need privacy (work meeting)	**HOW DO WE HELP? (GAIN POINTS)** ✓ We provide an upmarket, on trend art café with seating areas suited to social and casual work catch ups ✓ Our team are friendly and greet regular customers by name ✓ We are Mary's 'go to' coffice and social hang out

IDEAL CUSTOMER AVATAR

If we contrast this now to a law firm that has decided to target a tech start-up entrepreneur as their ideal client avatar, it would look quite different. Their avatar might be John. He might be:

- Age: 22 to 35 years
- Gender: male
- Domestic situation: single, no children
- Residence: renting, inner-city
- Occupation: tech start-up founder
- Income: will currently be minimal in the start-up phase with very, very high potential
- Activities: he's likely to be tertiary educated and he's likely to be very focused on business development. He

may be fitness-oriented and he's definitely going to be tech-oriented

1. His goals and values.
- John is likely to have a smaller circle of friends and largely within the tech or entrepreneur arenas.
- He'll have minimal income now but with very high potential.
- He values time efficiency, is intelligent, and processes complex information very quickly.
- He values knowledge and researches matters well before he seeks advice.

2. Where does he hang out?
- He'll be on socials and information sites, but very different to those that Mary would be on.
- He may be on Reddit, Stack Overflow, Medium, Cora, Discord, LinkedIn and possibly Twitter.
- He may well be a regular at cafes, but they won't be the ones that Mary goes to.
- He may be fitness-oriented, likely to be a gym or a runner.

3. His wants and needs, or his pain points.
- John is going to want quality legal advice at a high level.
- He will have done his research to a high degree before he seeks help.
- He will need assistance with setting up his company, with contracts, with IP protections and patents.
- He may well value connections into venture capital partners.

4. How do we help? Or the gain points we offer.
- Well, this particular law firm provides a team of lawyers with high-level knowledge in a variety of areas.
- They have several lawyers with an interest in and connections to the tech start-up community.

- They've purchased specific software systems to assist in this area.

As you can see, John and Mary's avatars are very different – in particular, from a marketing perspective, where they hang out is different. John is not going to respond to an advert on Facebook or Instagram. He is likely to not even have a profile on there, but he will be sourcing knowledge from a variety of very different platforms.

This law firm would need to position themselves as knowledge experts on some of these more niche social media and news platforms. If John sees regular blogs or posts demonstrating a high level of industry knowledge, he's much more likely to contact that particular law firm. Remember that John lives in a virtual world, and so the location of his law firm is of minimal significance to him.

Humanising your ideal customer in avatar form allows you to understand them more completely, in particular, their behaviours, needs, wants and pain points. It allows you as your Marketing Manager, to craft your business to meet their needs.

TARGETING YOUR MARKETING DOLLAR

As mentioned, the critical element here is to understand where your ideal clients hang out so that you can target your marketing effectively. You could market to Mary through carefully curated imagery and targeted promotions on Facebook and Instagram, while for John, building a brand as a legal knowledge expert for the tech industry, writing articles on Medium and LinkedIn, and participating in chats on Reddit, Stack Overflow and Cora will be more effective.

Around 1900, John Wanamaker famously said, 'Half the money I spend on advertising is wasted. The trouble is, I don't know which half!'. Over 100 years on, we are still in the same situation. A study by Alex Partners recently showed that global consumer product companies waste roughly $50 billion, or more than *half* of their collective spend, in digital marketing and trade spending. The survey found that half of the digital advert spend showed either negative return on investment or ROI was not measured at all. It's crazy that in 100 years of marketing we haven't improved our understanding as to how to get the best bang for the buck of our marketing dollar. Drilling down on client avatars makes a huge difference to how and *where* you should spend your valuable dollars.

AVATARS CAN BE GROUPS

Avatars are different for different businesses. For a physiotherapy practice, an ideal client avatar may be a young athlete with a sporting injury, but it also may be a medical practice that refers young athletes with sporting injuries. You would market to an individual athlete very differently to your marketing to a referring medical practice – and you should create an avatar for both.

One of my clients, a high end, boutique legal firm, had a very active presence on Google Ads, but, whilst it was targeted by geography to the relevant location, it was otherwise a scatter gun approach. We workshopped their ideal client avatars with their team, identifying half a dozen or so key avatars, including young home buyers requiring conveyancing, small business owners needing contracts and advice, corporates requiring employment contracts and employment dispute guidance, and workers with personal injuries claims.

Understanding these are all ideal clients for particular elements of the business is the first step. Understanding that you market very differently to a 25-year-old first home buyer than you do to a mature corporate with an employee issue is a critical element in refining the existing marketing spend. We were able to target social medial adverts and very specific Google adverts to make their marketing dollar significantly more effective, and their client engagement from digital marketing has increased dramatically.

I worked with a large client with multiple offerings in the entertainment space, including hosting functions and events. They have a fairly traditional older existing client base and we recognised that we need to appeal to younger demographics to provide growth, longevity and future security for their business. We created ideal client avatars for their existing clients, but also for a range of new, younger and corporate clients that would bring money and new lifeblood to their business. We were able to build a range of service offerings that would be more appealing to this newer client database, including setting up multiple, styled photo locations for those famous Insta-shots and quiet lounge areas for some of their older clientele that prefer a more traditional environment.

We instigated targeted food and beverage offerings, including specific events that would be more attractive to the younger market. This has dramatically changed their membership base and grown their offerings so they're now a much stronger and more sustainable business.

Remember, blanket marketing is wasteful and most businesses – Big or Little – don't have money to waste! Once you've drilled down into your ideal client avatars and personalised them to the extent we have discussed, you can ensure your product and service offerings are attractive for your avatars. And now that we understand who they are and where they hang out, we can market to them effectively.

> **ACTIONS YOU SHOULD TAKE AFTER READING THIS CHAPTER:**
>
> 1. Think about the ideal customers or clients for your Little Business and create your ideal client avatars.
>
> 2. Identify where they hang out and plan your marketing spend to target them more effectively.
>
> 3. Track the ROI on your marketing spending to be sure it is not being wasted.

Chapter 6

ROLES, GOALS AND PROCESS

CULTURE

The Gallup report, the *State of the Global Workplace* reports that 71% of employees in Australia and New Zealand are not engaged at work. This is worse than the global average of 67% and a sobering statistic indeed! Worse still, just 14% of our employees report that they are actively engaged in their job, showing up every day happy and with the enthusiasm and desire to be highly productive. Staggeringly, 15% are *actively disengaged*. Not only are these people unhappy at work, but they're often determined to undermine their boss and/or their fellow team members. But the vast majority of our workforce, 71%, simply fall into that *not engaged* category. They show up each day, but just do what's necessary to get through that day, and no more.

Building a strong culture where we engage our team and bring them into creating the shared goals for the business can make the world of difference in terms of employee and employer happiness, satisfaction at work and ultimately, workplace productivity.

This starts with the work we have already been building on – having a **Big Little Business on a Page** and engaging your team in workshopping your values, purpose, pillars and foundations. It also centres around your **Big Little Business Organisation Chart**, to ensure you spend time with that metaphorical People Manager hat on, asking yourself the strategic questions: 'How are our people?', 'Do I have the correct people for a high-performing team?' and as we will deal with now, 'Do I have robust and accurate roles, goals and processes in place to support my team to do the job they need to do?'.

All these questions are relevant and important, even if you are a microbusiness or sole trader. You need to consider how you and your team function and if all these support systems are in place. As we grow your Little Business, we need structure in place BEFORE we employ more people.

Building a positive culture begins with employing people with the same values that you have and building mutual respect. Technical skills are necessary for some roles and beneficial in most, but I will always select a team member based on attitude over skill when it comes down to the final selection. Skill (professional qualifications aside) is something that can be taught in the workplace if the person has the right attitude, but teaching attitude is a far more difficult thing altogether.

I regularly run cultural and strategic 'Reset Days' with clients, where we meet with the whole team for half a day or so. We review what the business has achieved in the past three months, then we goal-set together for what we would like to achieve in the next three months, actively asking the team for their improvement ideas and what they would like to work on. Engage with your team in this manner and they are much better equipped and motivated to help you achieve those goals. Additionally, they will have great ideas that you as the business owner may be surprised and delighted by. Your team will have a different perspective and often see things that we as business owners do not.

My formula for people management success goes something like this:

- find the **best people** that you can
- give them clear direction as to what their **role** is within the business
- give them a compelling and inspirational vision of your business and what you want them to achieve – **the goal**
- train them well with clear **processes** that are within their capabilities
- **empower them** to achieve the business and their individual goals using their skills and talents
- provide regular and timely **feedback** based on the agreed goals
- **value them** and reward good behaviour
- then **get out of their way** and don't micromanage them!

THEY JUST WON'T DO AS THEY ARE TOLD!

Managing a business is more about managing our people than the business itself. Get that right and the business will take care of itself – but get your people management wrong and it can be distressing and disastrous for all parties. One of the most common frustrations business owners face is managing their employees. 'I just want them to do their job,' they say. 'My staff keep making the same mistakes over and over.' And the classic, 'It's just easier if I do it myself'. My response to that is always, 'It may be easier the first time and the second time, and maybe even the third time, but by the tenth time, it's certainly easier if you had trained team members to do that for you'. The key is having clear roles, goals and processes, training effectively to those processes and having accountability so that employees will execute appropriately.

Most businesses take on their first employee before they have any systems or processes in place. We are busy, we need an extra pair of hands. We put out an advert, we interview, employ our best prospect, give them a brief training and expect them to know what to do from there.

But what is obvious to you in your business, is not necessarily obvious to somebody that hasn't ever done it before. We may find that new employee is not performing to our expectations, sometimes we get rid of them, get another person on board and repeat the same process over. When I speak to a business owner that says, 'My staff just won't do what I tell them to do,' I ask, 'Who's fault is that?'. They look at me blankly and say, 'It's theirs,' and I say, 'No, no, it's **yours**'. It's critical that we have appropriate processes in place to allow us to delegate work to our people and to allow them to be able to perform their duty effectively.

Most position descriptions, if businesses have them, are very transactional. They detail the tasks that an employee is to do. The business owner or team leader may run through this with the employee at the initial phase of employment, and then that document is filed away and forgotten, often by both the employer and the employee, unless there's a problem. We need to humanise position descriptions, and in particular, need to look at three key elements – the roles, goals and process.

ROLES

There is often quite a discrepancy between what a business owner thinks their employee should be doing, to what the same employee thinks is their role. Having clarity is critical to avoiding confusion in the workplace. Often a person may be taken on in one role, but as they and the business grow, their position changes – but the position description is not updated. Position descriptions should be reviewed annually or earlier if it is apparent that the role has changed.

A good position description will cover off on the role in terms of key responsibilities and duties. For each area of responsibility, detail the work standard that is required.

This might look like:

Responsibility 1: To manage the daily operations of our office for XYZ Catering including handling initial client enquiries, arranging venue bookings and completing catering requests for the kitchen. The employee needs to have a high level of computer literacy, be proficient in scheduling and be able to work independently.

Work Standard: All client enquiries are to be responded to within one working day. At the end of each working week, all catering events for the following week must be finalised.

GOALS

The most important thing in the role or the position description is the **goal**. What is the point of employing this person? What is their purpose within the business? This is usually the piece that's missing in a position description. There's a big difference between saying to an administration person that, 'Your role is to answer the phone, do the typing and make appointments,' and saying, 'Your role is to help our company fulfil its purpose to provide expert financial planning services and to help provide our clients with financial freedom'.

The goal for every position description should be in two parts:

1. To help you fulfil your business purpose from your Big Little Business on a Page. Every single team member is there to help you as a business, achieve your purpose.
2. A more specific purpose statement directly for their role. It might be to delight each customer with quality food offerings as a chef, or for a reception role, 'You are the face of our business and the purpose of your role is to make our clients feel welcome, comfortable and relaxed when they arrive'.

PROCESS

The next element is the **process**. Many businesses operate without any specific formalised processes, assuming their team members will know what to do, often with minimal training. Have a procedure for each critical task that employees undertake in your business, to ensure they are done consistently and to your required standard. Having a process also provides a framework for difficult conversations if a team member is not performing as required.

For those of you that have children, you will quite likely have the issues of wet towels left on the bathroom floor, or dirty clothes left lying around the house, or any number of dirty glasses left on the kitchen bench instead of being placed in the dishwasher. Typically, it's the behaviour we want to get rid of, not the actual child. Although, at times, there may be exceptions to this rule! It's the same with our team members. The cost of replacing people is enormous in terms of advertising for re-employment, training new team members, et cetera. If we can train the existing people we've already got, then we are in a much better position. So, having sound roles, goals and processes allows us to *blame the system* rather than the human being. It also allows us to identify if a system is broken, so we can fix it and retrain the existing team members, satisfactorily.

The master of all business process is McDonald's. They have built a global empire based on consistency and standards. The Big Mac that you buy in your local McDonald's will be the same as the one you will find in any city, anywhere in the world. Many years ago, I took my entire team to McDonald's and their manager ran us through a training program. We were then able to go into their kitchen and with just 20 minutes of training, we could follow their process and produce a Big Mac pretty much identical to one that you would purchase anywhere. McDonald's have evolved their systems and processes to the level that they can take an inexperienced 14-year-old and have them trained as a functioning employee in a very short period. This is a very efficient and very consistent business model and one that we can all learn from.

So, where do you start with developing your processes? Start with the things that are irritating you right now. What's not working well and causing problems? What are the things you find yourself saying to your team over and over and over again? If you're having to repeat yourself, it means that there is no system or the system you have in place simply isn't working. Who is the best person to develop a system? The person that is already doing that role. Ask your administration person to write a system for making the bookings, or to answer the phone, or any of the other many jobs that they would do through the day. Ask your best salesperson to write a process based around the sales system so that you have consistency amongst all of your team. Processes should be simple to follow, ideally one page per process, minimal words and in dot point, sequential form. Test your process. Get a new team member, someone that doesn't work in that area to run through it and try and make it as simple and easy to follow as possible. This is about building a turnkey business that runs effectively now and also increasing the saleability of your business when you're ready to exit.

GENIUS ZONE

When looking at the roles for your people, make sure that you play to their strengths. Everybody has a 'genius zone', an area that they enjoy and an area in which they perform well. Whilst we all need to do tasks that don't inspire us at times, your team (and business) will perform better if you can play to your employees' genius zones as much as possible. Employees that are engaged at work perform better – 21% better according to *Gallup*. What's not to love about that? This may be as simple as identifying an administration team member that has a knack and love for marketing and engage them to assist in this area, or a retail assistant with a flair for merchandising who can take the lead in creating displays when a new product comes in.

I have on several occasions redeveloped segments of my business to suit the genius zone of an individual team member. In each instance, it has been to suit highly valued and highly productive team members that have felt the need for a new challenge. If a team member is feeling restless in their role and you don't provide some extra stimulation for them, they are likely to leave. There are certainly times that a team member has outgrown a business and it suits both parties to split respectfully, but if you have a valuable employee and you can create a new challenge within your business for them, then you should consider that as an opportunity to provide growth for both them and the business.

In one instance a valued and long-standing team member of mine wanted to provide a new service to our business. This was in an area of her passion and well within her genius zone. She came to me with an idea and we evaluated it together. The idea was consistent with our business values and purpose but would require financial investment from me as the business owner and would add an additional pillar to my business. Wearing each of my metaphorical C-Suite hats in turn, I investigated the proposal:

- CFO – The hard costs were in the order of $25,000 to provide the training, building modifications and equipment set up for this new venture. It was anticipated we would break even in 6-9 months and be moderately profitable thereafter. Our CFO (me) was a little concerned about the opportunity cost of taking this person out of their normal role for effectively a day a week into this new and less profitable role, but if it was manageable overall the CFO was comfortable to proceed.
- COO – There was some work involved in setting up the infrastructure and systems to run with this new element of the business but very little was required operationally aside from the time required for training and set up. Our COO (me) was happy to proceed.
- Marketing Manager – This was a new addition to our business and would require marketing to promote it. It was considered desirable to our current client base and was likely to be well received. Our Marketing Manager (me) was excited by the opportunity! (Marketing Managers are excitable people and generally excited by most opportunities I find!)
- People Manager – The main demand was on the time of this one team member. We had additional staffing

requirements to cover her workload during training and set up and for her ongoing staffing of the new service. A new set of roles, goals and processes for this element of the business was required. Our People Manager (me) and was happy to proceed on the basis that this team member's work satisfaction level would increase dramatically, and she was a valuable asset that we wanted to retain within the business.

- CEO – On assessing each of these facets, it was clear that this was an achievable option. This was a niche service and would be attractive to a segment of our existing clients, plus, it would bring in additional clients to the business that we could offer our existing services to. It was never going to be highly profitable but would certainly cover itself and also serve the purpose of keeping this team member motivated and retain her for the business. The risk analysis dictated that we would train two or three team members in this service so that if the key team member did choose to leave the business at a later time, we could still offer this service and use the infrastructure we had invested in so that we did not end up with a 'white elephant'. The end decision was to proceed, and it allowed me to grow the business as well as to retain that team member and reinvigorated her passion for all areas of the business.

ACCOUNTABILITY

Drawing from each team member's position description and in combination with your business strategic and financial goals, you should set clear key performance indicators or KPIs for your team (and for yourself). Individual KPIs are essential goals for the team member and offer the business a way to measure their performance objectively. They are an important way to manage your employee's performance and outputs and give you a tool for fair accountability conversations. It allows you to understand the employee's performance and to direct and redirect where appropriate. It also allows you to put in place a fair reward system for high performance if that is warranted.

Like any goal, the KPI should be SMART:

- **Specific**: there must be clarity over what you are measuring and what the expectation or benchmark is.
- **Measurable**: ideally easy and quick to measure.
- **Achievable**: a goal that can be reached but not a *given* that they will achieve just by showing up. A KPI should be a slight stretch but something that can be achieved if they are following the processes correctly.
- **Relevant**: to the business growth and also to the team member's role.
- **Time-Limited**: are we measuring this KPI daily/weekly/monthly?

Have a look at the drivers of performance for your business and each team member. Some KPIs are designed to grow your business and some are designed to grow the person, to assist with their professional development. What things would benefit the business if you could do more of them? What things would benefit the team member's development if they could improve? Set benchmark targets for the KPIs and they now become valuable as a development tool. It takes a while to determine the correct KPIs for your business. You may run with one set of KPIs for some time then change them up to focus on a different area of business and professional development.

KPIs should be easily measurable and you (with your People Manager hat on) should check in with each team member daily, weekly or monthly, discussing their KPIs and importantly, celebrating the wins when they achieve them and discussing what they can do to improve in the periods that they don't reach the numbers.

Some examples of individual KPIs that can be useful:

- Number of leads, prospects or contracts signed
- Number of blogs or social media posts published
- Number of calls to clients or customers served
- Customer satisfaction rating (measured by surveys)
- Average sale per customer (for retail and service industries)
- Total $ sales or efficiency % (billable vs. non-billable time)
- Task completion rate or time spent per task
- Gross profit (GP) of sales (high-profit vs. low-profit items)
- Outputs – items/products/reports produced
- Cost management (as a % variance to budget)
- Food (or other product) wastage
- Days outstanding of a particular measure (responding to clients, outstanding accounts, et cetera)

You might report KPIs in a dashboard layout or have a pass/fail system where they hit the KPI or they don't. You could also consider a traffic light system which is helpful for grading performance. In this system, green is good (KPI is achieved and everyone is happy), red is bad (KPI is not achieved and is at an unacceptable level, so performance management is required) and yellow is 'room for improvement' (KPI is not achieved but the employee can improve this themselves by following the processes that are in place).

REWARDS

There are many rewards for an employee doing a great job. A sense of satisfaction is one, and a smile or thank you from a customer, supervisor or the business owner is another. Having a job and a regular pay cheque is also a reward. But a little extra can go a long way. Rewards can be fun – a box of treats, a bunch of flowers, movie tickets or a dinner voucher – or monetary, from a $20 team incentive to a $100 or more bonus in their pay. Good team members want to be challenged to grow and develop their careers, so speak regularly to your team about what their goals and aspirations are and how you can help them.

Human beings intrinsically like to achieve, most people want to do a good job. Tell them what good behaviour looks like and thank and reward them when they do it. Employ the person with the right attitude, engage them in the business, share your purpose, give them the tools and structure they need to do it, and get out of their way and let them get on with it!

ACTIONS YOU SHOULD TAKE AFTER READING THIS CHAPTER:

1. Review your human resource structure with your People Manager hat on. Think strategically about your employees. Do you have the right people in the right roles for optimum performance?

2. Review the roles, goals and process for each of your team members and tweak when necessary.

3. Set KPIs for each team member based on the key responsibilities and work standards in their position description.

Chapter 7

WHAT'S HOLDING YOU BACK?

TIME

You know those people that seem to pack so much into their day? They may be a colleague, a friend or a respected member of your community. A good friend of mine is a strong businesswoman. She has four children and a loving husband. She runs a thriving business, serves as a director on several boards, spends time giving back to the community on a voluntary basis, and always seems to be cool, calm and collected. What's her secret? She does not waste a single minute of her busy working day. She sets a structure and importantly, she *sticks to it*. Does she work a million hours? No. She's a stickler for finishing her work on time and spends mornings, evenings and weekend time with her family and friends.

CONCENTRATION IN A DIGITAL WORLD

We all have the same amount of time each day, 24 hours, 1,440 minutes, or 86,400 seconds. It's what we choose to do with those valuable hours, minutes and seconds that makes all the difference. But it's difficult. We have so many distractions to deal with, more so these days than ever. We are connected every minute of the day. Our phones are often the first thing we check when we wake up and the last thing we touch before we go to sleep. We check our phones every 10 minutes throughout the day according to global tech company Asurion. Messages will ping, emails will come in, social media posts will pop up demanding our attention.

This constant fragmentation of our time and attention has become our new normal but how does it impact our ability to get stuff done at work? More and more experts are telling us that repeated interruptions significantly reduce our concentration and efficiency. Dr Glenn Wilson, a psychologist from the University of London found the most damage to the efficiency of office workers was done by an almost complete lack of discipline in handling emails. The study found there was a compulsion to reply to each new message as they arrived, leading to constant changes in direction of the thought process, which inevitably tires and slows the brain. 'If left unchecked, info-mania will damage a worker's performance by reducing their mental sharpness. It's a recipe for muddled thinking and poor performance,' said Dr Wilson.

One of the secrets to managing our time is diary blocking. Schedule time in your diary for specific tasks and stick to it. This includes blocking specific time to manage emails and return phone calls, rather than constantly checking each email as it arrives, interrupting the flow of work that you would otherwise be doing. It also includes carving out time blocks for those C-Suite strategic thinking questions that we have covered in Chapter 2. Now, this is easier said than done. It's a discipline, a habit, and like any habit, the more you do it, the easier it gets. Professionals like doctors, lawyers, and accountants are generally very good at scheduling time and being disciplined within that time block. They run their days by appointment. If something is in their diary, it will typically get done.

Different businesses have different demands. If you are a retailer and you work in a busy shop, it's very hard to carve out the administration or strategic time that you need. You may need to schedule your diary blocks and arrange staff coverage for that period or rearrange your diary, so you start an hour earlier one day a week, before those interruptions for the day begin. Remember back in Chapter 2, when we discussed Big Little Business Organisation Charts and diary blocking? Schedule time in your diary for strategic thinking and it will grow your business. Once strategic thinking becomes a habit, it becomes second nature. You will cherish and defend that precious, strategic time, adding enormous value to your business.

PRIORITY MATRIX

Given that we can't magically add an extra couple of hours to our days (as much as we might wish it), it then becomes how we choose to spend those 24 hours, or more particularly, how we *prioritise* that precious time. Dwight Eisenhower was the 34th American president, from 1953 to 1961. He was an army general and he called it as he saw it. One of the many legacies that he has left is the Eisenhower or Priority Matrix. This simple chart can be life-changing in terms of scheduling your time effectively.

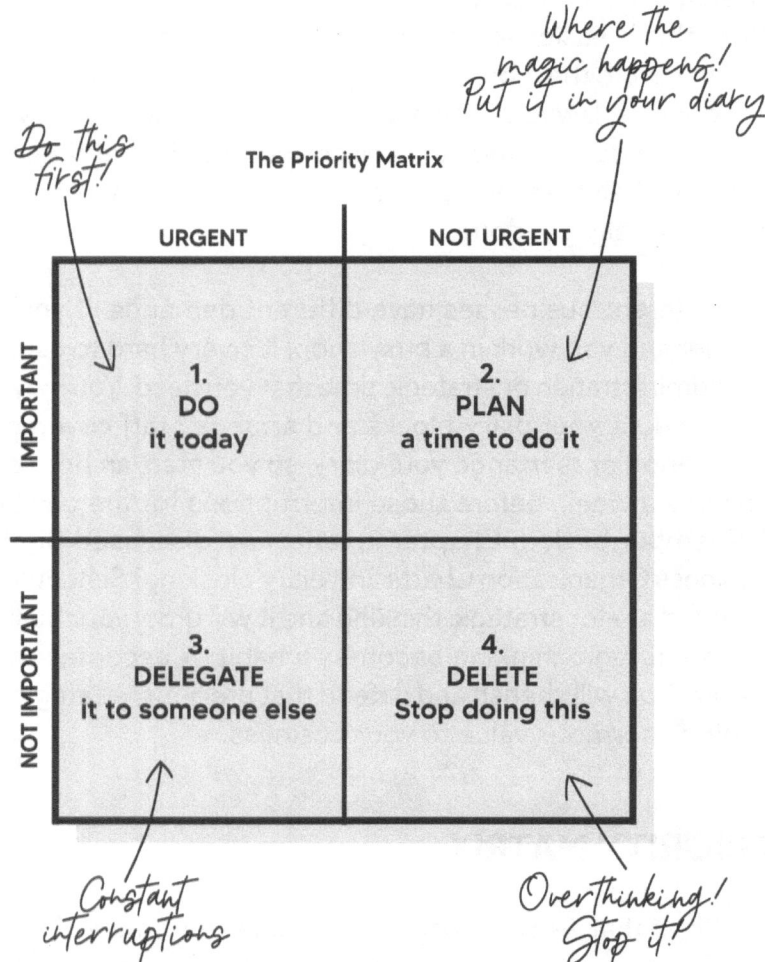

THE PRIORITY MATRIX

The Priority Matrix is split into four quadrants of urgency and importance, the **urgent** quadrants run down the left side and the **important** quadrants are across the top. The order in which you should prioritise your time is as follows:

1. **Quadrant 1: Important AND Urgent – DO**
   - Deadline projects – *do these NOW.*
   - This might be an urgent customer request, a quality control issue or a report that you need to get out by the end of the day.
   - Most people are pretty good at actioning Quadrant 1 tasks.

2. **Quadrant 2: Important but NOT Urgent – PLAN**
   - This is the strategic work that you know you should get done but there is generally no deadline to it, so it's easy to put it off and off and off.
   - Quadrant 2 is where the magic happens and where Big Business thinkers hang out, thinking strategically and planning for the best way forward. When you put on your metaphorical C-Suite hats, you are functioning in the all-important Quadrant 2.

3. **Quadrant 3: NOT Important but Urgent – DELETE, DELEGATE OR PLAN**
   - These are distractions that typically serve somebody else's needs but not your own.
   - Quadrant 3 is the big black hole for all the *helpful* people out there. Those of you that put other people's needs ahead of your own and wonder why you can't get anything that matters to you done.
   - This might be other team members looking for reassurance, asking you to solve their problems for them or asking questions that they could find the answer for themselves with a bit of thought. The daily interruptions and distractions, non-important phone calls, emails or non-important meetings.
   - If you can delete the items in Quadrant 3 then do so. If not, can you delegate them to someone else? If not and they need to be done, they probably are important but

not urgent (to you). They belong in Quadrant 2 and you should plan to do this at an appropriate time.

4. **Quadrant 4: NOT Important AND NOT Urgent – DELETE!!!**
- All you *perfectionists* get stuck here – overworking a project, tweaking a report long after it needs to be tweaked, to the point you are adding little if any value to the end product.
- *Busy work* is another version of this, being busy all day but not actually producing an outcome probably means you are stuck in Quadrant 4.
- Set yourself a time limit to complete a particular task and if you find yourself reworking it over and over, you need to ask: will the result be that much better for it? Or has the work you have done already met the requirements?
- Getting distracted and surfing the web or personal social media whilst at work are other examples of Quadrant 4 distractions.
- You need to delete tasks that are not urgent and not important!

One of Eisenhower's famous priority quotes is, 'What is important is seldom urgent – and what is urgent is seldom important'.

Quadrant 1 tasks need absolute priority: if something is urgent and important, you need to get that done. People are typically very good at doing urgent and important things – you have an important meeting scheduled so you're going to make time to attend. If you have an urgent client or customer request to attend to by the end of the day or any other deadline project, you will generally make it happen. But after Quadrant 1, we often find ourselves drifting into Quadrant 3, attending to tasks that are urgent, but NOT important, or as Eisenhower would say *not important to us*. These are low-value tasks, interruptions, distractions, non-important phone calls or emails, or non-important meetings.

PUT YOUR OWN MASK ON FIRST

As we are instructed each time we take a flight, in an emergency you should *put your own mask on first*. If you don't look after your own needs, then you are not functioning optimally to be able to help others.

As a business owner, your level of responsibility is to do first what is in the interests of your business. Not what is in the interests of any particular individual, but that which will further the purpose of the business. I coach business owners to take full responsibility for their business in all regards. I have often seen Little Business owners make poor business decisions as they focus on the needs of an individual team member or individual client or customer, above the greater good of the business as a whole. In an ideal world, the decisions we make are of benefit to all parties *and* the business, but in the real world that does not always happen. When there is a conflict, you must ask yourself, *what is in the best interests of the business?* Refer back to your Big Little Business on a Page values and purpose, and the answer will guide your decision-making.

Eisenhower would say Quadrant 3 tasks that are urgent, but not important, typically serve *somebody else's needs* and do not further our own. Consider if you are serving your business needs or those of someone else when you find yourself in Quadrant 3.

Conversely, Quadrant 2 tasks that serve **our** business needs, are the very things that tend to get pushed back and forgotten because they are not perceived as urgent. This should be the second priority area that you spend your time in. Quadrant 2 is where the magic happens. These are all the important tasks that will impact positively on your business in the future. But they are easy to put off. You may have scheduled an hour in your day for blue-sky thinking, but other more *urgent* issues may pop up, business bushfires that need your attention or a team member needing direction (often on a matter that they are quite capable of dealing with themselves). Do not allow yourself to get caught up in Quadrant 3, putting out someone else's bushfires, when you need to be back up above the line in Quadrant 2.

Quadrant 2 is where strategic thinking lies and is, arguably, the most important Quadrant in the Priority Matrix. But because things like strategic planning, improving your systems, exploring new opportunities and relationship building tend to not have deadlines attached to them, it's very easy to put them off because we are *too busy*. But as we learned earlier, this strategic thinking time is what will be the biggest turnaround for your Little Business. The single most obvious difference between a Big Business and Little Business mindset is how they value and prioritise Quadrant 2, strategic thinking.

If you find yourself getting off track, you should refer back to your Priority Matrix and ask yourself, are these tasks important, or are they simply urgent, but not important to you? Do they serve the needs of others rather than bringing you closer to your personal and business goals?

If you are frequently distracted by Quadrant 3 interruptions from your team, asking for instruction on what to do, then we need to go back to our roles, goals and process, and make sure our team are adequately trained and empowered to make decisions for themselves. This, of course, is strategic Quadrant 2 work that you need to have in place already. If you find your interruptions are urgent, but not important to you, then you need to delegate them to somebody else who can do these for you, plan for them for a later time or simply delete them.

Quadrant 4 is not urgent and not important and, of course, you have to wonder why you would do these at all. This can be overworking a project, procrastination or getting side-tracked surfing the web or social media when you should be researching for a work project. There is certainly a place for rest and relaxation, but not during your working day when you have other work scheduled. So, save these tasks for your downtime at the end of the day. Junk email falls squarely into Quadrant 4. Not urgent, not important. From time to time, go through your emails and unsubscribe and delete anything that falls into this Quadrant. Set up rules in your email folder to manage this. Non-important email can be a massive time-waster.

In terms of dealing with those interruptions throughout the day, *people will treat you the way you allow them to treat you*. If you allow employees to come to you repeatedly for small matters, that they really should be able to do themselves, they will continue to do so. You must refer back to roles, goals and process. Do you have the right process in place for them to know what to do? If so, refer them back to the process. Sometimes team members will come and ask for your approval because they think that's what you want them to do. Work on building a culture of competence and confidence where your team are empowered to think for themselves.

Once your team know what to do and have the confidence to work and make decisions for themselves, they generally will do so. This will free you up for that all-important strategic work. Empowering your team to deal with issues themselves, frees you up to spend more time working on the important, but not urgent strategic work.

Understand that Quadrant 2 strategic work is where the true value of a leader is. This is the growth area and allows you to put strategies in place to ensure your business is running optimally.

This is the work that allows you to *prevent* bushfires rather than waiting until they occur before you try to deal with them.

THE PLAN

To be clear, you should guide your time through the Quadrants in order. Quadrant 1, then 2 then 3 then 4. Do not get distracted by Quadrants 3 and 4 until Quadrant 1 and 2 are completed!

Once you start to analyse tasks before you dive in and do them and consider which Quadrant they belong to, you'll find prioritising comes naturally to you and you will value your time more critically.

My friend, the businesswoman, like all those people you know that seem to pack everything into their day with ease, has got the Priority Matrix down pat. She spends her time in Quadrant 1 and then Quadrant 2. Quadrant 3 is delegated or dealt with by her team members before it even gets to her desk. Quadrant 4 is not even a consideration.

Where do you spend most of your time?

ACTIONS YOU SHOULD TAKE AFTER READING THIS CHAPTER:

1. Go to my website, www.jaynearlett.com.au/resources, and download the Priority Matrix that you can customise to your common tasks. This will allow you to quickly identify the triggers for you that are the time-wasters. Once you find yourself doing them, delegate or delete.

2. Practise prioritising your tasks before you tackle them. Do the important ones first, not the easy ones. This is the key to dealing with procrastination.

Chapter 8
HOLD YOUR COURSE

NEW AND SHINY

The world is not short of good ideas for business but sustainably executing them is another thing altogether.

If you're good at what you do, and you open a business, you will typically do very well initially. People like new and shiny. If a new coffee shop opens nearby, you're likely to give it a go, friends will invite you to check out a new restaurant and you might pop into a new retail shop to see what they have on offer. A new business typically gets an initial flush of trade from clients or customers who are *checking them out*, which can be a false predictor of what is to come. If you continue to do well and the money starts to roll in, you may be tempted to expand rapidly. There is a fine line between being ready to capitalise strategically and being the *fool that rushes in where the brave fear to tread*. Expanding too soon is a recipe for disaster, which I know only too well.

When I initially established my first business, I grew rapidly and expanded too soon with no strategy or systems in place to manage that growth. It almost broke my Little Business. I was struggling. I had sleepless nights. I didn't know how I would survive. I had not yet learned to be a Financial Detective. I had not done the numbers to fully understand the financial impact of what I was doing. I was caught up in the importance of growth for growth's sake, rather than about sustainably driving the business. It was a painful lesson financially and emotionally.

STRATEGY IS KEY

A client of mine owns a microbusiness, she was a sole trader when we first started working together. During our first couple of meetings, we set her a six-month strategic goal to grow and pivot her business into a more sustainable enterprise. We set the strategy together, but it was her job to execute it, which she did with enthusiasm and drive. In just five weeks she achieved the goals that had been set for six months! She was buoyed by the excitement of the rapid expansion of her business and was ready to employ her first team member. I pulled her back into line, and we steadied her business. She knew how to work the business under her own steam, but she had not put any systems in place to allow her to employ, train and direct a new team member with any degree of surety.

We went through the procedures that we covered in Chapter 6 and held her business steady for several months while she put in place the required processes – the systems and procedures that would allow her to employ additional team members with some certainty that they would be able to function at the high level that she required. At the same time, we worked on business growth strategies to ensure she had sufficient revenue opportunities to be able to cover the increased costs of becoming an employer. Once she had all this in place, she was able to then put on her first team member, and together, they grew her business further and stabilised again, before she went through the same process a second time. We led her business through periods of growth followed by consolidation, allowing her time to reassess her business needs and direction, before embarking on the next phase of growth, then again consolidation.

GROWTH FOR GROWTH'S SAKE

Growth is good, but it needs to be part of a bigger strategy. Begin with the endpoint in mind: what is the grand plan for your business? What does growth mean to you and what is the *purpose* of growth? For many business owners, growth is about increasing the number of employees or perhaps moving to larger premises or opening additional outlets. Ultimately, growth is about profitability, but there are many ways to increase profitability without increasing your business costs. This is where some solid blue-sky thinking with your metaphorical CFO and COO hats on can be invaluable to explore other opportunities such as reviewing your price structure, your cost structure and your operational efficiencies. When you are ready to expand and employ new team members, make sure your People Manager has robust roles, goals and processes in place to allow them to be onboarded efficiently.

Understand that rapid and continuous growth of a Little Business is unsustainable for most. Businesses need periods of consolidation to be able to adjust to their growing needs. The exception to this is large, well-funded businesses that can consolidate and adapt constantly throughout the growth phase and manage the collateral damage along the way.

For many Little Businesses, continued, rapid growth will be too much to bear, and you will reach the breaking point where your systems and procedures will fail you. Instead of looking for constant growth, plan for periods of rapid growth followed by consolidation periods whereby you take a breather, re-evaluate and put in place those systems and procedures you need to ready the business to take off again. This will provide you with a much more sustainable model for your future.

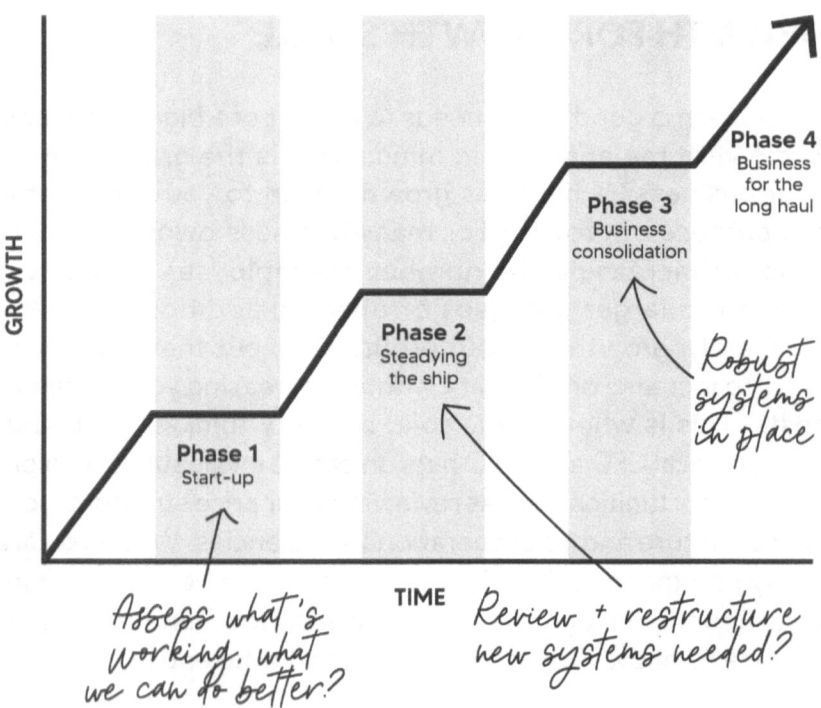

GROWTH-CONSOLIDATION GRAPH

Another client of mine working in the health industry is a very accomplished businesswoman, although she has certainly had her ups and downs over the years. In the early stages of her business growth, before we were working together, she had rapid uncontrolled growth because she was very good at what she did and she said *yes* to every opportunity without evaluating the operational requirements. She was growing without any strategy which is like racing a car in the dark with no headlights.

From the outside, the business looked great, but it was out of control, and she knew it. I walked into her office one day to see her sitting on the floor, crying. I scooped her up, and after we debriefed, we put in place a solid strategy that has seen her manage this growth.

We set a plan. We engaged her employees in decision-making, and we built a strong and positive work culture. We hold her team accountable to the KPIs that they help us set relevant to their individual roles, goals and process. This Little Business had 50% growth the first year we worked together, followed by two successive years of 30% growth year on year. A phenomenal achievement but one that has been controlled in spurts to allow us to manage that growth effectively. There was a period at which the business had outgrown the current premises, and with a team of more than a dozen people, they were bursting at the seams. They were ready to move into new premises, but again, we put a halt on that. We worked as Financial Detectives to set budgets to see what level of revenue would be sustainable with the new and increased rent that we would have in a new premise. We halted that business for 12 months while we grew internally, knowing then that when we did move to the new premises, we were financially viable and sustainable for the long run.

Look to create a growth/consolidation, growth/consolidation model. Use the consolidation phases to strategically plan and restructure the business as needed for the next phase to keep control of it so that you don't burn out. Make sure you build your personal as well as your business resilience along the way.

Growing businesses constantly is exciting but exhausting. If you're not ready for it, it will break you.

LOOK AFTER YOU

Look after yourself at all times, but particularly while your business is growing. Take regular breaks to recharge, find the things that energise you. For me, spending time in nature and frequent short holidays, often camping with no mobile or internet connection, does the trick. I couldn't fathom working 12 months without a break. I learned very early on in my career that multiple short breaks through the year are what recharges me. We will typically take about six family holidays a year, but some of these are simply long weekends. It's rare for me to take more than two or three weeks break in one hit, and if I do, that's for a major adventure holiday. Everyone is different so find what works best for you. For some, taking a few days to rest at home is bliss, while others will need to get away. Some people recharge with exercise and others by curling up with a good book. Whatever it is for you, make sure you know what recharges your batteries – and have your People Manager schedule it in your diary regularly!

In between your scheduled breaks, make sure you practise healthy habits that assist you to operate at peak performance levels. Generally, this will include regular exercise, getting a good night's sleep, healthy eating and quality downtime. Make sure you know what you need for you to function at a high level. Burning the candle at both ends and running yourself into exhaustion is not going to have you operating effectively. Write a list of what you need to do to function at your best and refer to it whenever you need that little extra support.

THE OPPORTUNITY OF A LIFETIME

The opportunity of a lifetime comes around once every month or so.

The risk of growing your business too fast, too soon can lead to disarray, high-stress problems, and sometimes, business failure. Jumping at new and shiny opportunities that are not consistent with your values and purpose statement is a great way to split your focus, and you end up trying to be everything to everybody and doing none of it particularly well. You will lose your niche focus and lose your appeal to your clients or customers.

Understand that there is a need to evaluate opportunities as they come up in business **as long as they're consistent with your values and your purpose statement**, but do this in your strategic timeframe, not that which suits others. Is this opportunity consistent with your master plan for your business and your life? Does it move you further to your ultimate goal? If not, pass it by. Another opportunity will come along at a better time for you.

You may be thinking, *Shouldn't I take advantage of every opportunity in business while I can?* The answer is no, not if your business is not ready. Not every opportunity is a good one. Make sure you have the back end of your business in order with solid strategies, sound financials and a solid plan before you take each step forward. One well-executed plan is going to be more beneficial than 10 poorly executed ones that are likely to fail.

Similarly, don't be tempted to open a second or third business just because you're busy. It certainly can be a great plan to duplicate an already successful business, but it can also cannibalise the business that you already have. Opening a second business should not be the first thing that you consider. Think about adjusting your prices, increasing your staffing, including work from home options, increase your online capabilities, et cetera. Market forces dictate that if you're crazy busy, you see more clients or customers by increasing your staffing, extending the hours of operation, or you put your prices up. Opening another office or shop and increasing your fixed costs is not always the right plan.

Never turn away the perfect opportunity at the perfect time, but don't grasp a new and shiny one just because it's there. Plan your growth and be prepared so you can manage it fully and capitalise on the perfect opportunities when they come knocking.

ACTIONS YOU SHOULD TAKE AFTER READING THIS CHAPTER:

1. Review the growth and consolidation phases your business has had over the years.

2. Review where you're at, at this point in your business journey. If you're coming off a big phase of rapid growth, it may be time to pull in the reins for a short period while you consolidate your systems and procedures to make sure they're capable of taking you to the next level.

Chapter 9

ROLLER-COASTER JUNKIE

LEARN TO LOVE THE RIDE

When you decided to go into business, you bought yourself a ticket on a roller-coaster ride, whether you knew it or not.

Now I happen to *love* roller-coasters, literally and figuratively. I think I had my first roller-coaster ride as a child at a seaside fun park in the UK. I love the anticipation and excitement of riding up the hill of the roller-coaster, knowing that at the top, there will be a magnificent view soon to be followed by the thrill of the fast ride down. There would come a low where I would catch my breath, but I knew that at the end of every low, there was going to be another up. There was going to be another high.

And so it is in business, as indeed it is in life. Often when we go into business, we get that initial flush of growth, it feels wonderful and we want that to continue forever. But the reality is that the thrill of your new business doesn't continue forever, the reality of hard work kicks in, you will get your first *overly demanding* customer or your first *really difficult* employee. You will have a competitor with a big marketing budget open up nearby or you will have a great idea for your business that just doesn't come off. You will have ups and you will have downs.

If you're going to be a survivor in business, you need to understand the natural ebb and flow of business as well as the occasional bigger dips that you will face, and you need to learn to love the ride.

THE LITTLE DIPS

I will divide our business roller-coaster dips into three categories:

1. **The normal ebbs and flows of the business.** You will have busy times and slow times; you will have competitors challenge your market share and difficulty obtaining stock or finding suitable employees at times. It can be challenging to manage the slow times or shortages of resources but use the tools such as your cash flow forecast to help you navigate through these periods. Put on your metaphorical C-Suite hats and have your CFO closely manage your financial obligations, your COO tighten up those loose processes for maximum efficiency and your Marketing Manager market the heck out of your business to get more clients or customers in the door.

An important side note on marketing here. Remember we said marketing is your *rainmaker*, its purpose is to increase revenue for your business. It is also a big money pit if it's not used correctly. Many people spend money on marketing because they know that they should and tell themselves it's about *branding*, but ultimately your marketing spend should increase your revenue. However, without a solid strategic plan behind your marketing and some method to measure its effectiveness, it can be a massive waste of money that would have otherwise gone to your bottom line. IF (and that's an important if), you are using your marketing correctly and it generates revenue, you should *increase* your marketing when times are tough as you will have the confidence it will bring people into your business. Marketing should be a revenue-generating investment, not an expense to the business that you feel you should cut when things get tough.

2. **The little dips.** These are the mini crises, which feel like a big crisis at the time. This can be the loss of a key team member at the *worst possible time*, or if you are a sole trader – sickness or an accident that puts *you* out of action. It can be a forced requirement to relocate at the end of your tenancy if the landlord wants the premises for something else, or a major competitor opens up with a big marketing budget determined to dominate your market. If you are a professional in a service industry like health, finance or law, it may also be a government or major supplier audit that uncovers a problem or the threat or reality of a lawsuit.

Concerning staffing, it's important to remember that if you employ people, they are more than likely to leave your business at some stage. It's also important to recognise that the business is its own entity and it is bigger than any one person, even you! It's critical to put on your People Manager hat and ensure those robust roles, goals and processes are in place which will allow you to recruit and train replacements as smoothly as possible. Never have one person in your business being the only person that holds all the knowledge in a particular area. This is your business intellectual property; you need to ensure knowledge is held by several people and the important processes are documented for business resilience and sustainability.

Competition is generally not as much of a problem as people think. Shopping centre retailers will know that a good centre manager will carefully curate small clusters of similar shops. You do not want to be the only fashion retailer in a shopping centre, customers like choice, so being part of a cluster of similar (but not too similar) retailers will bring more customers to the shopping centre and ultimately to your store. In times of increased competition, revisit your Big Little Business on a Page, centre on your purpose and focus on your foundations, the things that allow you to deliver to a high standard on your purpose.

3. **The BIG dips**. Some of these are REALLY big and every business should consider how your Little Business could cope in a disaster scenario. Understanding business resilience and building a contingency plan *before you need one* is the key to riding out the storm. Understanding and prioritising contingency planning is another key difference between Big Business and Little Business thinking.

THE BIG DIPS

So, what do the bigger dips look like in business? I'm not talking about the peaks and troughs of the normal business cycle; I'm talking about crisis management here.

I've become somewhat of a disaster or crisis management consultant over recent years. Australia, like the rest of the world, is seeing an increase in natural disasters. I assisted businesses to recover from the disaster that was Tropical Cyclone Debbie that impacted Queensland and New South Wales in 2017. Then we had significant floods in Northwest Queensland in 2019, about a third of the region's population was impacted by these floods. At the same time, in other parts of the country, there was severe and widespread drought. Later on in that same year, it seemed our whole country was on fire with devastating bushfires. Just as we thought we were coming through all of that and were pleased to see the end of 2019, we were hit globally with COVID-19 in early 2020.

Whilst COVID-19 is a disaster on a global scale that we haven't experienced before, we have certainly had devastating pandemics throughout the world in recent times, such as SARS (2002), Swine Flu (2009), MERS (2012), Ebola (2014) and of course history is well peppered with devastating pandemics throughout the ages. All of these had significant and widespread impacts.

From a business management perspective, how can we expect the unexpected? History and global trends give us strong clues.

ADAPT AND PIVOT

Disasters are by their very nature disastrous, but they are not something that we should be surprised by and we can take steps now to plan for a possible future disaster, whatever that might be. Whenever we're faced with a crisis or a major downturn, preparation is key. Businesses that had been previously impacted by cyclones, drought, floods and fire, and had recovered, were better placed to manage the shutdowns of COVID-19 as they had learned valuable resilience and contingency lessons from their earlier experience. We can't plan for every single crisis that might or might not happen, but we can and should have a crisis or contingency plan which focuses on business resilience and sustainability.

Come back again to your Big Little Business on a Page and understand the importance of having multiple pillars. If, for example, you are a single pillar business, like a full food service business, and you are forced to close, whether it be from a flood or a cyclone or a pandemic, you are going to be in a world of pain. But, if you can adapt and pivot your business, so you have full food service as one pillar, takeaway as a second, home delivery as a third and in-home catering as a fourth, then you have added resilience to your business. If you're forced to close down your physical food service premise for a period, you have other offerings available to you as a revenue source.

A major part of contemporary business resilience is utilising technology to its fullest and having an online offering of some sort. A training company, for example, that relies totally on face-to-face training, should explore adding virtual training as an option. This might not work for all of their offerings, but I am yet to find a training company that could not benefit from introducing some element of online training. A beauty clinic that relies on face-to-face delivery should be taking advantage of technology to provide online booking and online retail sales of their products. Service industries should be looking at telecommunications as an option for delivery of some of their meetings and almost every business can benefit from exploring digital offerings in their industry.

I hear constantly from businesses that their business is *different* and that what works for one industry won't work for theirs. Absolutely, every business *is* different. That's what makes you unique, but any business in this day and age that does not have a serious online offering is putting themselves at risk.

Sadly, 40% of businesses don't reopen after a major business disruption, and of those that do, another 25% fail within the first year. We want to keep your business within those that survive and indeed thrive. So, let's have a look at the strategies we can put in place to achieve that.

BUSINESS RESILIENCE PLAN

When is the best time to build a business resilience plan? *Before* you need it. Business resilience planning is largely about creating steps that can be used in response to a crisis. There are three stages to this:

- respond
- rebound
- rebuild

When we rebuild, we should adapt and pivot to return with a stronger, more resilient business than we had before. Let's start by looking at a business impact analysis. We analyse the threats and the risks to our business based on the likelihood of them happening and the impact it would have if it did happen.

The Business Impact Matrix is a simple chart that allows you to quickly identify which risks are more likely to have a significant impact on your business, so you know which ones to prepare for first.

	Minor	Moderate	Major	Critical
Very Likely				
Likely				
Possible				
Unlikely				

Low impact — Moderate impact — High impact

BUSINESS IMPACT MATRIX

What would you do if you had to close your doors today due to a natural disaster? What if a key employee suddenly quits, if a major client doesn't renew their contract or if your business burns to the ground?

If you have several employees in your business, set up a crisis management team. In times of crisis, people look to the leaders for direction, and you as the CEO or owner of your business are the obvious leader. But if you're unavailable, who would be your second in command? Who are the other key leaders within your business that would help you manage through a crisis? It's important to think about setting up a management team that has diversity. You might want a frontline person, a younger person, and an experienced person, all of whom will give you the diversity of thought and allow you to build a robust plan.

Think about each potential crisis after evaluating its risk on the Business Impact Matrix. What would happen if we had to close our business for a period – would we survive? Why or why not? Which business areas drive our revenue and how could we pivot and adapt if one of those areas was compromised? Break down each of your pillars, into their critical functions and analyse the risk for each of these. This could include your ability to see clients or customers face-to-face, keep your doors open, work in a virtual world, maintain 24/7 customer service and how you would interact with a remote team should you all be having to work from home.

Once you've gone through the process, it's important to reconnect all the pieces with the workflow. Your business is a machine and it needs to be well oiled so it can run. Every piece of work, every system needs to flow into the next one. Having workflow charts, process maps or mind maps can be useful. Your COO and operations people will shine in this role. When you're working through the system, ask yourself, where are the blockages in the pipeline? And how can we relieve these? The goal of your business resilience plan is to allow you to maintain operations in any scenario, and your plan should include updated workflows, checklists, organisation charts of your crisis management team, documents outlining the most likely risks and scenarios, mock tests or exercises and walkthroughs of crisis management planning, statistics, data, and likelihood of risks for your business. You can glean a lot of information regarding risks and likelihood of these risks from insurance companies. Outline each employee's role within a crisis, identify the critical functions and create contingency plans to deal with them.

Please don't think because you've been in business for many years, that you don't need a crisis plan. The old saying, *it's all okay until it isn't* is why people find themselves unprepared, like a deer in the headlights when a crisis hits.

Throughout COVID-19, we saw businesses that thought they were recession-proof in a world of pain. Typically, medicine and healthcare services have been seen as recession-proof businesses. People go to see the doctor because they *have* to, not necessarily because they *want* to. Health care is a necessity and not part of discretionary spending, and as a result, many healthcare businesses operate without a resilience plan. However, during COVID-19 surgeons were unable to operate and many medical practices were empty. People perceived them to be a hotspot of infection and just simply didn't go. Some medical businesses were able to pivot and adapt to telehealth and other delivery models very rapidly, and this stood them in good stead to withstand the crisis.

If you do have to close your business for some time, it's critical to continue engaging with your clients and with your team. This is not a time to cut your spending on marketing. Remember your marketing is your rainmaker and can bring new clients or customers to your door. Keep contact with your clients or customers, so that when you can open again, they remember who you are. If your business can pivot and adapt, you need to have provided updates and communication with your clients or customers, so that when you are ready to reopen, perhaps in a slightly different format, they are there for you. Similarly, with employees, it's vital to stay in touch. Working from home can be a very convenient mechanism and works well for some team members, but not for all. Keep the communication lines with your team open and be sure to use technology for video calls, to keep some element of face-to-face communication going. Even in a virtual world, remember the human element of assisting your business through a disaster.

THE PEOPLE FACTOR

It's important to recognise the emotions of loss. It is normal to grieve for what we have lost. Particularly those who have gone from crisis to crisis like floods, bushfires, cyclones and earthquakes. We grieve for the loss of what we had planned. Stages of grieving may include:

- **Denial, disbelief**: This doesn't feel real, it can't be happening to me.
- **Anger**: In its mildest form you may be fearful and worried, perhaps developing to short-tempered, or full-blown angry.
- **Seeking to understand**: Why me, why is this happening?
- **Depression:** In its mildest forms it can be sadness, overwhelm or a feeling of helplessness through to full-on anxiety and dark depression.
- **Acceptance**: It is what it is. We can't control our external circumstances, but we can control how we react to it. We need to move through to the stage of acceptance before we can move on and fully deal with the problem.

You cannot solve an emotional problem with logic as much as we may try. Not everyone moves through each of these stages and they may or may not be sequential, but assisting people through to acceptance where possible, can be helpful.

The value of having a disaster management plan in place **before** disaster hits is that you are prepared. You have a plan; you'll be able to stay in a much better state of mind as you go about dealing with this situation. It is very difficult to plan for a disaster when you're already in one. The emotions, the grief and the confusion you will experience will make it very difficult to process the most basic of information. Having a plan in place and a crisis management team within your workforce allows you to respond, rebound and work towards rebuilding much more effectively than if you didn't have this.

Being hit with a disaster when you have NO plan, means you will struggle to cope. When disaster hits, you'll spend valuable time processing and planning, which could have been done in advance, and you'll be more severely impacted than if you had already built your business to be resilient.

ACTIONS YOU SHOULD TAKE AFTER READING THIS CHAPTER:

1. Read the ultimate guide to business resilience at www.jaynearlett.com.au/blog

2. Look at the pillars of your business, and make sure you have multiple pillars that can be strengthened during times of adversity.

3. If you don't have some sort of online offering to your business, get it happening now!

Chapter 10

YOU CAN HAVE IT ALL - JUST NOT ALL AT ONCE!

MY WISE MENTOR

A wise mentor of mine taught me many years ago about whole-of-life goal setting. He has lived this himself and having sold his business interests some years ago, is now semi-retired, although he still works occasionally as a consultant, imparting his many years of wisdom to others. He and his wife now live on a tropical island, cruising in their boat whenever the fancy takes them, travelling the country to visit family and friends and holidaying around the world, whenever they wish. He certainly wouldn't say that he has it all or that life has been easy, but he has got a good handle on what the important pieces of life are, and quality of life is a core value for him.

SILO GOAL SETTING

Most people don't engage in formal goal setting exercises, and when they do, they tend to do it in silos. We might goal set for our exercise, deciding to exercise three times a week, perhaps writing this down and then beating ourselves up when we can't fit it into our busy schedules. Or we might do some financial goal setting and set ourselves a plan for our personal income and perhaps for investments in the future. We might goal set for what point in time we would like to have children, or what our career or travel goals are, et cetera.

The difficulty with goal setting in a silo is that something else always pops up. As we have discussed before, we all have just 24 hours a day, 1,440 minutes, or 86,400 seconds every single day. We have a lot that we want to cram into each of those days. When we goal set in silos and we don't take into account all the other elements of our life, we are doomed to fail.

Many people goal set dutifully once a year. Gyms pump out their highest membership sign-ups in January. The gyms are pumping, but they have a rapid drop off in February and again in March. Only 50% of people who have bought an annual membership regularly attend the gym according to a study by the University of California. Great for the gyms, but not for those people that are unable to keep up the commitment that they made in a silo.

WHOLE-OF-LIFE GOAL SETTING

So, what is the answer to goal setting success? It is to have a look at your goals for your life in *context*, taking into account all of the things that are important for you.

Let's have a look at a whole-of-life goal setting exercise. Take a sheet of paper and draw a wide column on the left. Across the bottom, write your current age, I'm going to assume that you're 35 years old. At the top of the paper, you're going to write the age at which you might come towards your end of life. You might pick 85 or 95. Down the bottom at your current age, we want to list off all of the things that are important to you. Now, this might include:

- income
- net worth or personal assets
- health
- fitness
- education
- career
- family relationships
- friend relationships
- spirituality
- travel goals
- and anything else in life that might be important to you, which of course will be different for everybody

Beside each of these important elements of our lives, we want to quantify where you are in your journey on achieving these goals right now at this particular age.

Income and net wealth are easy to measure, they are numbers. We can quantify those simply. But for all of the others, which are perhaps a bit more nebulous, we can grade them out of 10. How is your health? You might be sitting at an eight if you are reasonably healthy, but know that you need to do more exercise, or reduce your alcohol intake, or eat better. Or your health may be a six if you have a family history of health issues and you are not maintaining your weight or your fitness. Whatever it is, grade it out of 10, and move on to the next one.

How are your relationships with your family? Is it an eight or a nine, are you doing pretty well? Or is it a five or six with some difficulties that need to be addressed? Is it a similar story with your relationships with your friends? And where is your career? You might be flying pretty well, an eight or nine, or perhaps you have lots of goals left to achieve and you might be a five or a six.

Once we have ranked our current status, we then will move up to the top of the page. At age 85, how would you like to see yourself sitting on these important elements? We might like to think that we would all be a 10 out of 10 but stop and think about what this might look like. You'll typically find that your relationship-type values and your health values are more important now than your career. If you're having difficulty visualising how this might look for you when you're 85 years of age, think of your parents and your grandparents, or people in your network that are this age. What do they value most?

The finances are interesting to look at when you're 85. You will find that you will be consuming much less money than you probably think at this age. Again, have a look at parents and grandparents and what they tend to spend in retirement. Most of us will spend quite a lot in the first couple of years after retirement, but as time progresses, you may well find that travel is less appealing than you thought it would be. You have bought that nice retirement car that won't get driven a lot, and you probably have already travelled in the early years to most of the places that you want to visit. The reality is most people will spend a lot less in retirement than they think they will. Factor that into the net worth that you need and the income that you think you need in retirement. For many people, they overthink this in their thirties and forties. The reality of what they need for retirement is significantly less than they estimate.

We now have our current scorecard and then our end-of-life desired scorecard. What do we do next? Well, let's break this up into five-year periods. If you're 35 years now, 40, 45, 50 and so on. For many of you, there is a long time to go between where you are now and where you want to be. The reality is that most of our goals are quite achievable.

WHAT WILL YOUR LIFE LOOK LIKE IN FIVE YEARS?

Where do you think you might be in five years from now? Typically, we overestimate what we can achieve in 12 months, but *vastly* underestimate what we can achieve in five years. Have a good think about what your life was like five years ago. You'll probably find it's dramatically different to how it looks now.

There are ebbs and flows in life just as there are in business. There are times in your life that you will have to focus, as a business owner, on your business and perhaps put some other things aside for a short period of time. That may mean that we don't focus so much on our family and friends, or we don't focus so much on our sporting or exercise activities for a short period.

Keep your precious goals, the ones that you want to be a 10 when you are in retirement, quite high. We don't ever want our family relationships to drop down to a two. It's going to be very difficult to bring them back up to a 10 again from there. But if your exercise or fitness goals, travel goals and perhaps even your friendship goals drop off for a period, that's something that can generally be picked up again when you have a little more time. Understand that your early years of business are the times that might well take a focus, but it doesn't have to be like that forever. Building a sustainable, systemised, strategic business, as we have discussed throughout this book, is what will take time in the early years, but will *give you more time* in later years.

There will be times in your life that are your key money-making years, times that are key family years and times that are key career or education building years. Have a look at your whole-of-life goal setting plan and schedule in where you think your key focus needs to be and what milestones you want to achieve along the way.

Revisit your whole-of-life goal setting page regularly to keep you focused. Are your actions taking you closer towards your goals or further away? Remember that these are your goals, you own them and can change them if you need to. I revisit my whole-of-life goal setting each January instead of making New Year's resolutions. In the early years I would tweak my five-year goals slightly as my life path changed but I find the precious goals, my 10 out of 10 goals are always consistent. I know what my precious goals are, and I nurture these constantly.

For each of my pregnancies, I have taken 12 months off work. Having a systemised, stabilised business has allowed me to take those times where my family became a 10 and a top priority, and my business dropped down to perhaps a five or six, as I knew that the systems in place would allow it to run well without me.

Trying to be everything to everybody and trying to be a 10 out of 10 in every single element of your life every single year is just not going to work. You'll put a lot of unnecessary pressure on yourself, and you'll feel like a juggler with too many balls in the air trying to manage it all.

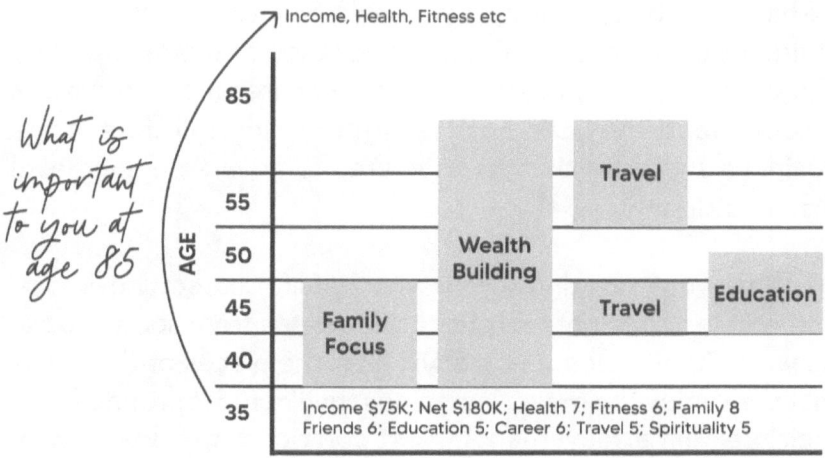

WHOLE-OF-LIFE GOAL SETTING

YOU CAN HAVE IT ALL – JUST NOT ALL AT ONCE

I work with a lovely couple who are in business together with about half a dozen team members. They are a dynamic couple in their late thirties with three young children. They're going great guns in their business, growing and developing, but were burning out trying to handle it all. We went through this whole-of-life goal setting process and scheduled some systems to relieve the workload on them, as they needed some time to focus on getting their children settled at school. There were some health issues with one of the children that necessitated an increase in family time for that period.

We worked on the profitability of the business, understanding the key levers to increase their revenue, and that allowed us to employ another team member to relieve one of the business owners to spend more time with her children. There was no drop in the bottom line for them because of the strategy that we had put in place earlier on, so they're able to achieve a whole-of-life balance that suits them at this stage of their lives. They know that in years to come when the children are a little more independent, they can both return to being full time in the business and drive that revenue area to an even higher level than it is already.

When you're looking at your whole-of-life goal setting, just be aware of the highlight reel effect that we see from social media. As we all know, most people will post the pieces of their lives that they enjoy the most. The things they're most proud of, and their greatest achievements. Most don't post the drudgery of daily life, thankfully. It's easy to feel that everyone else is having a perfect life and a 10 out of 10 in every element of their lives. As we all know intellectually, this is simply not true, but emotionally it can have an impact sometimes thinking everybody else has it all and we're the only ones struggling.

This simply isn't fact. Everybody has ebbs and flows in their lives. Everyone struggles in some element of their life. Life is not a competition. It's there to be enjoyed, and when we pace it out over our lifespan, we can do just that.

ACTIONS YOU SHOULD TAKE AFTER READING THIS CHAPTER:

1. Sit down and do whole-of-life goal setting. Give yourself an hour of some blue-sky thinking. You and your partner, if you have one, should do them separately and then sit down and discuss together.

2. See how your plans will work together and how you can set yourself some goals for which parts of your life you need to focus on career, which parts you need to focus on family, which parts you need to focus on travel, et cetera.

Chapter 11

Best Coffee Ever!

DON'T REINVENT THE WHEEL

Fundamentally I'm a lazy person. That doesn't mean I don't achieve a great deal through my days. I can be highly productive. What it means though, is that I am constantly looking for ways to get things done quickly, especially the stuff I don't like doing. I prefer to get it in and out so I can get on doing the things that I enjoy more. I get stuff done.

So, what does it mean when I say I'm lazy? It means I'm constantly looking for ways to improve the *efficiency* of the things I do. If a task might ordinarily take an hour to do, I'll find a way to do it in half that. I wear my metaphorical COO hat and constantly analyse systems and procedures to see if there's a better way. And I cut out unnecessary steps to get things done quickly.

My laziness means I'm incredibly efficient. I don't believe in reinventing the wheel, and I like to learn from other's mistakes rather than make them myself. That just seems like the most efficient and sensible thing for me to do.

When I first set up my business some 25 years ago, mentoring was not a thing. There was very little in terms of support for small businesses in any way, shape or form. There were no government grants to help you get your Little Business established. There were minimal business supports or education available and it was a matter of sink or swim. Fortunately, society and governments now recognise that small businesses are major contributors to the general economy, and there are many more support systems in place – in particular, business mentoring.

FOR THE PRICE OF A COFFEE

Back when I was getting my Little Business off the ground, I knew that I was making mistakes, I just didn't know what to do about it. I was smart enough to recognise that reinventing the wheel continuously made no sense at all. I sought out people that had experience in the areas that I was having difficulties with, and I asked for their advice. I would arrange a time to bump into them at a business function, or sometimes just give them a call and ask them if I could buy them a coffee in exchange for half an hour of their time. Sometimes people would say no, they were too busy, and they would let me down gracefully. But surprisingly, the majority of times people would say yes. I got to meet and spend time with some incredible people that I admired very much. And every single time I did that, they would impart some little gem of wisdom that would be useful for me.

Most of my mentors over the years have been very informal. Many of them would be surprised to think that I regard them as a mentor. They might be a business contact, a colleague or friend that I have had occasional chats with.

Nowadays, there is an enormous amount of support available for you to develop your business and you should take advantage of educational opportunities and grants to help you build a strong and resilient business that contributes to our community.

Additionally, I strongly suggest that you seek out mentors to maximise your efficiencies and learnings in the areas that you need it most. The mentor-mentee relationship is a special one and very much personality dependent. Not every mentor and mentee will gel, even if they appear on paper to be a perfect fit from a knowledge perspective. There are formal and informal mentoring relationships, and there are paid and voluntary mentoring relationships. All have their place, and all can add great value to you.

Look for a mentor that has the right personality to blend with yours. The best mentors are people with a giving nature that connect with you on a personal level. They will challenge you and you will learn from their years of experience. I understand that some people like to make their own mistakes, but it just does not seem like the most efficient way to learn! You certainly *can* do it for yourself, but *you don't have to*. You can do it quicker and with a lot less pain if you have guidance from somebody who already knows how to do it.

One of the many benefits a mentor can provide for you is valuable connections to other people that might add benefit to you on your career journey. Mentoring is often a long-term relationship with connections lasting long after any formal mentoring has finished.

INFORMAL MENTOR

As a starting point, think about people in your community, maybe that you know, or maybe just people that you know of, that have done what you want to do - that have achieved in the areas that you want to achieve in.

They may be a friend or a colleague or a friend of a friend. They may be somebody that you have met at a business function, or they may be somebody that you just know by reputation. Either way, there is no downside to approaching them to see if they will have a coffee with you and impart a little bit of wisdom. If you are going to go down this path, you need to firstly not be upset if they say no, because to be fair, most successful people are busy and prioritise their valuable time. They may offer you a phone call rather than a coffee, which would also be valuable. Be very aware of the rules of engagement in such an informal mentoring relationship. You must be very respectful of the mentor's time and also of their intellectual property. And you may well ask questions that they don't wish to answer, so be respectful of where the boundaries may be and don't be offended if they decline to discuss some topics with you.

But typically, people like to help other people and the most successful business people have quite likely been in your shoes at one time or other. Many of them would be willing to have a cup of coffee with you and impart some pearls of wisdom that may be of some value.

FORMAL MENTOR

Moving on from that, there are many organised mentoring groups available. Check out your state government's business page. They are likely to have some mentoring programs available, which may be free of charge or at a minimal cost. I am a regular mentor in the Queensland Government's Mentoring for Growth program, which has a bank of experienced volunteer mentors. There is no cost to the participant to have an hour-long session with one or several mentors. The group sessions are fun. They can be a little bit like a *Shark Tank* set up where the mentee arrives with a specific question that they wish to ask, and a panel of mentors can provide some incredibly valuable insights, challenges and advice in a very short period.

Many business organisations will have more formal mentoring groups available, which may be ongoing for several months. Some of these are paid and some of these will be free of charge. Find a program that works well for you.

IT'S LONELY AT THE TOP

Aside from sourcing a volunteer mentor, you may choose to employ a business mentor or coach for a specific project or for an ongoing business growth development relationship. Typically, a six-month mentoring program will give great value. A short project-based mentoring session may solve a particular problem, but to get ongoing long-lasting benefits, plan to engage a mentor for a six-month contract or beyond. Many business owners will employ a business coach or mentor to work beside them permanently. They typically slot in beside you, into your C-Suite structure, perhaps as a *parallel CEO*, another you, another set of eyes.

One of the single biggest issues that people don't realise when they go into business is that it's lonely at the top. There is nobody to bounce ideas off and all of the pressure is on you to make the decisions. If you don't have a good solid support structure around you, that can be very difficult. And certainly, a paid mentor or business coach can provide that for you. In the same way that athletes benefit from having a sporting coach beside them throughout their athletic career, business owners benefit from having a business coach beside them.

Understandably businesses sometimes worry about the cost of paid mentoring or business coaching. But the return on investment should be many times over what you pay. Like marketing, business mentoring or coaching shouldn't be seen as a cost to the business, but a revenue earner for you. In fact, 71% of Fortune 500 companies invest in formal mentoring programs for their leadership team and their employees. They know that their return on investment is well worth it.

So, what makes a great mentor? Someone that genuinely wants to help others succeed. Someone well experienced, but not necessarily in your field. Having a different perspective, an outside set of eyes can be invaluable. One of my clients is an engineering company with a national footprint and several offices across Australia. I am not an engineer, although my father was one. One of the great values that this company will tell you, is that I came with a different mindset and a fresh set of eyes. There is a real problem with *groupthink* in some industries where they don't have the diversity of skillset. If lawyers are trying to mentor and coach other lawyers, that's the only perspective that they can give. Bringing somebody in from a commercial background with a different mindset gives a different perspective and you get away from the groupthink mentality. My engineering company often talk about the helicopter view that I would give of their business and the humanistic element that we were able to bring. We worked a lot with them on resilience, following the flooding disaster in our region, and that held them in good stead for the resilience required to deal with COVID-19.

My own mentoring journey has been from a variety of informal mentors. Some of these were close friends working in different industries to me. One was a school principal. One was a senior executive for a very large company. And one was the business owner of his own major company who is now retired. None of these people would probably identify themselves as my mentors and they may also claim that I mentored them. That was the beauty of our relationships, that it was a two-way street and we would share information and learn from each other.

Even now many years on I have two wonderful friends that I catch up with for very long lunches several times a year. We're all high-level businesswomen, all in non-competing fields. We get together infrequently and solve the problems of the world over a few glasses of wine, but also talk quite openly about our own business concerns and issues. And we openly mentor and coach each other. This informal peer mentoring group is easy to set up with friends or colleagues in non-competing industries.

Whichever route you choose, the benefits you can gain from mentoring are invaluable.

ACTIONS YOU SHOULD TAKE AFTER READING THIS CHAPTER:

1. Make a list of three potential mentors that you would like to have a coffee with and approach them one at a time.

2. Look up any government or business industry mentoring programs that might be of value for you.

Chapter 12

PLAN B

HOPE IS NOT A STRATEGY

Plan B gets a bad rap, somehow seen as inferior to Plan A – the original. But having a Plan B is very much Big Business thinking and is what will get you out of trouble time and time again. Little Business thinking is that their great idea will come off and be a great success, because ... well, because it's great!

In reality, the best-laid plans don't always come to fruition. There are many things out of your control that contribute to the success or otherwise of your business or any particular project that your business might initiate. As we have learned before, the world is not short of great ideas, but it takes a lot more than a great idea, a great product or a great service to become a success.

When is the best time to develop a Plan B? *Before* you need it. Hope is not a strategy.

PLAN B FOR PERFORMANCE MANAGEMENT

Business management is more about managing people than the business itself. People management can be tricky and is a common pain point for both Big and Little Businesses alike. Discussing expectations with employees and having clear roles, goals and process is the first step towards creating a high-performing team and makes people management much smoother for all concerned.

However, from time to time, you may still find yourself with an underperforming employee. In this case, we may move into *performance management* to improve that performance and resolve the issue.

In an ideal world – using Plan A, you will have a few meetings with the team member, clarify the roles, goals and processes, identify where the problem lies and rectify the situation. Remembering we are looking to get rid of the behaviour, not the person. Blame the system, not the person, identify where the system has fallen down, let's fix that and keep that person as a part of the team.

It may be that we have changed a few things in the workplace, or perhaps the old process is no longer working and needs to be rewritten. Or maybe the team member is not following the process because they did not fully understand it, or they did not realise it was part of their role to do this task.

In any of these situations, you would fix the system if it needs fixing, rewrite the process if needed, retrain the team member to that process and we will now have a high-performing team again.

However, we are dealing with human beings here and things don't always go to plan. The team member might not enjoy being *performance managed* and may quit suddenly, may not be willing to follow instructions or you may deem them not suitable for the role. Either way, it is preferable to have a Plan B in place *before* you take a team member into performance management.

To prepare for the possibility that a team member may suddenly quit or you dismiss them, your Plan B thinking would be:

- What specific tasks does this person do?
- Which of these tasks can an existing team member do currently?
- Which of these tasks can an existing team member do with some additional training?
- Which team member could take over in the short term if required?
- How can you provide the required training to upskill a replacement into this role?
- Do you have solid roles, goals and processes for this team member's role to assist a new person to slot into their position?

Now, we always hope that Plan A comes off, but if it doesn't, it's reassuring to know we have a Plan B in place.

NEW OPPORTUNITIES

Every business strategy for current and new opportunities needs to have a risk assessment. We covered risk in Chapter 9 with our Business Impact Matrix. We discussed considering the potential major risks to your business and prioritising them based on the *likelihood* of them occurring and the *impact* it would have if that did happen. This allows you to develop a **Business Resilience Plan** and to be prepared for future major crises.

But the Business Impact Matrix has a dual purpose – it can also be used for assessing day-to-day issues and is particularly useful for assessing new opportunities for your business.

Let's say you have a concept for a significant new offering within your business. It might be a new service or product line and might even be a new pillar for your business.

Using your C-Suite skills and wearing your metaphorical hats:

- your CFO will assess the financial impact
- your COO will look at the operational requirements
- your Marketing Manager will be excited by the opportunity (they always are!)
- your People Manager will assess the human resources required
- and you as the CEO, then take the overall view and decide if this is in the best interests of your business as a whole

Once you have assessed the project and decide to implement it, you will essentially have an action plan from all the considerations from your C-Suite evaluations – what the financial, operational, marketing and the people requirements are.

Understanding that the best-laid plans don't always work out though, run through the critical elements of this action plan and use the Business Impact Matrix to assess the impact of each element should it not run as anticipated. If you can identify moderate to high risks that would jeopardise your plan, now is the time to do some blue-sky thinking and consider what other steps you could take to keep the project on task should you need to.

Having a Plan B is what will help you to adapt and pivot quickly to keep your project on track.

ACTIONS YOU SHOULD TAKE AFTER READING THIS CHAPTER:

1. Create a Plan B for the loss of a key team member, or if you are a sole trader, for yourself. If you or a key team member were suddenly unavailable, how could your business manage?

2. If you have a new opportunity that you are considering, use the Business Impact Matrix to evaluate risks and plan ahead to mitigate them.

AFTERWORD

WHERE TO FROM HERE?

Following the Big Little Business thinking throughout this book will hold you in good stead for your business success, allowing you to grow your Little Business as Big as you want it to be.

To recap, the important elements are:

- having clarity on your business values and purpose
- building your Big Little Business on a Page
- understanding and then protecting and defending your pillars
- prioritising C-Suite strategic thinking – block it in your diary!
- drilling down into your profit centres and focusing on those that really make you money
- getting the best bang for your marketing buck by understanding your ideal clients or customers and keenly targeting your marketing
- learning to love your financials – or at least not being frightened to look at them!

- getting your metaphorical People Manager hat on and having solid roles, goals and processes in place *before* you employ people
- learning to prioritise your time so you can focus on the important things in your business – and your life
- understanding the roller-coaster ride that we call business
- not reinventing the wheel and seeking support where you need it, including mentoring
- AND always having a Plan B

I wish you all the best in your Big Little Business journey and I hope you enjoy the ride!

ABOUT THE AUTHOR

Jayne Arlett has lived and breathed business for over 25 years.

She understands most business owners are passionate about their businesses and experts in the technical aspect of what they do, but often lacking in understanding the mechanics of business which can not only prevent their growth but can be detrimental to their long-term sustainability.

As a highly sought-after and decorated business consultant and coach, Jayne guides business owners through the journey of discovery whilst learning to truly understand the back end of their business to help them grow.

Jayne has worked worldwide as an elite sports medicine professional with the Chicago Bulls, the Bears and the White Sox as well as Australian teams the North Queensland Cowboys, the Townsville Fire, Townsville Crocodiles and the North Queensland Fury FC. She is an Olympic and Commonwealth Games Podiatrist and uses the parallels of high-performing athletes and high-performing business to help Little Businesses grow.

Having run her own successful businesses in medical, retail, tourism and manufacturing, she built her Little Business into a Big Business with a $10 million turnover. She has had a parallel career as a board director working strategically with Big Businesses in excess of $1billion turnover. Jayne applies Big Business strategies to Little Businesses to help them thrive.

Jayne is an in-demand business consultant, presenter and author.

E: admin@jaynearlett.com.au
W: www.jaynearlett.com.au
LinkedIn: Jayne Arlett
Facebook: Jayne Arlett Consulting

BIG LITTLE BUSINESS ON A PAGE
Workbook

BONUS OFFER

Growing your Little Business into a Big Business begins with a dream, followed by a plan, a strategy and then the focus to execute that strategy.

It all starts with your Big Little Business on a Page. Use my free workbook to guide you through blue-sky thinking your business values, purpose, pillars and foundations to create your own Big Little Business on a Page. Everything you do in business is filtered through your values and purpose and your pillars keep you focused on what is important to your business success.

Download your free copy of the Big Little Business on a Page workbook at www.jaynearlett.com.au/ebook

admin@jaynearlett.com.au
www.jaynearlett.com.au
 Jayne Arlett
 Jayne Arlett Consulting

BUSINESS KEYNOTES AND WORKSHOPS THAT MAKE A **BIG** DIFFERENCE

With over 25 years of business and governance experience, Jayne brings an informative, practical and real-life perspective to your corporate or small business event or workshop, delivering quality and practical strategies that make a difference to the participants.

Delivering from real world business experience with honesty, Jayne connects with her audiences in an engaging but no-nonsense way.

Key topics include:

- Grow Your Big Little Business
- Find Your Inner Financial Detective
- Best Coffee Ever – the Benefits of Business Mentoring
- Roller-coaster Junkie – How to survive the Ups and Downs of Business

Get in touch to engage Jayne as a speaker or workshop facilitator.

admin@jaynearlett.com.au
www.jaynearlett.com.au

 Jayne Arlett
 Jayne Arlett Consulting

BUSINESS ON A PAGE
Online Learning

If you enjoyed *Big Little Business* but want to fast-track your business journey, get in touch to continue learning and growing.

Jayne offers personal Virtual Business Coaching worldwide and has a range of self-paced online offerings to help your Little Business Grow.

Get in touch to find out more about our online learning opportunities.

admin@jaynearlett.com.au
www.jaynearlett.com.au
in Jayne Arlett
Jayne Arlett Consulting

www.ingramcontent.com/pod-product-compliance
Lightning Source LLC
Chambersburg PA
CBHW021150080526
44588CB00008B/285